ISBN:	Hardcover	978-1734964554
	Softcover	978-1734964547
	Ebook	978-1734964530

This book was printed in the United States of America.

To order additional copies of this book, contact:

Shunduay LLC

1-818-649-9396

www.Shunduay.com

DEDICATION

To My dearest Tatay & Nanay of mine, in the midst of my misfortune; your memory is not painful to me, since the idea consoles me that fate had spared you of not seeing them, but if unexpectedly happy days should come to me, perhaps I should complain that you not had been permitted to reap the reward of my well-being.

About the Author

Born just two years before the Second World War, my life has been dramatically influenced by the war. I was born in 1937 in the wooden house at the foot of the mountain in Camonohan. While still unaware of what was happening around, WWII broke out in Europe and soon enough reached the Pacific. Japanese took over the provinces and municipalities of the Philippines, including my hometown—Panganiban.

I spent my early years in our farms by the mountain, avoiding the attention of the Japanese soldiers that occupied our town. WWII brought extreme poverty and difficulties among the townspeople, to which I was not spared. However, together with my family and neighbors, I soon learned to live with the terror of the war. Because of the chaos, we learned to appreciate what we had and exhibited exceptional camaraderie and unity.

I started my primary education behind other children of my age because the schools were forced to close until the Japanese were defeated. I started schooling at the age of eight, with nothing but improvised uniforms and school supplies. After the war, money and food became so scarce that attending school was already a remarkable feat.

After graduating from elementary, I paused my education for two years to help my father on the farm. Because of poverty, my siblings and I needed to take turns in helping in their family's livelihood. I attended CAIC, a high school in the town with a focus on agriculture and fishery. In class, we spent half of their day doing fieldworks on the farm or in the ponds.

But I defied the odds and finished his primary and secondary education with flying colors. I graduated with high honors in elementary and as a valedictorian in high school. Along the way, I also proved my character on top of academic excellence. Using my grades in high school, I received a 5-year scholarship from Araneta University. I took an undergraduate degree in Agricultural Engineering. Once again, I had proven my diligence and determination when I graduated with Cum Laude (Latin honors) in 1963. Not long after, I was admitted to the University of California, Davis, to advance my studies in Agricultural Engineering in the field of irrigation management and soil conservation. I was also offered a job as a graduate research assistant in the same department.

Other books of Frank

A Touch of Life: Real life story of the author during the darkest times of WWII in the Philippines (2nd Edition)

The Thing of Beauty Is a Joy Forever: A Colorful Life of an Immigrant in America (2nd Edition)

Pan American Flight #863 to Paradise!: From the Author's Small Town of Panganiban to the Vast Plains of America, Including Collection of Inspirational Poems & Other Literary Works Vol. 1, 2 & 3 (2nd Edition)

Frank's Magical Farm

Laughter in Disguise

Please visit my website www.frankadelarosa.com to know more about my beautiful life story.

CONTENTS

PREFACE

It has been almost a century since the Second World War happened, but despite a long time, the memories of the war remain inscribed in my memory. There are already lots of accounts about the battles and events of WWII, especially in Europe. But few, if not none, look at the impacts of the war to the typical people who were caught in between its participants.

I decided to write this memoir to show you what WWII meant to an innocent child. Born just a few years before WWII, this book contains the story of hardship, poverty, and terror. My town was home to our enemy, and fear was our constant companion. However, what differentiates this memoir from books with the same theme is that it also contains stories of camaraderie, love, compassion, and resilience, among others. While the war was going on, we were still able to see and appreciate the good things that surrounded us. I put into this book my adventures during and after the war—the happy, inspiring, and unforgettable ones. Through this memoir, I hope to inspire you to look beyond the challenges you are currently facing. Through the stories of my life, I hope to show you how obstacles—be it in the form of war, poverty, finances, or anything—should not stop you from believing that good things are yet to come. Know that you are bound to succeed as long as you put your heart and mind into your goals.

Chapter 1

My Hometown, Panganiban

Panganiban was a rather small town. Found in Catanduanes's northeastern coast, Panganiban was the home of my childhood memories, the earliest years of my life. It has witnessed the terror of the War, the resilience of its people, and the progress that followed the devastations.

The life in Panganiban was simple. During my childhood, we enjoyed no luxury nor financial wealth. In the eyes of the current youth, such life may look barren and gray, but having lived during that dark time of history, we found refuge in life's simplicity. It united us and formed unconquerable camaraderie. I must say that back then, we had a really close neighborhood. Everyone knew each other, and every family survived by supporting one another. Growing up, I enjoyed the company of the people in town. Despite the terrors of the War, Panganiban gave me the memories that I will forever cherish.

Panganiban was still young when World War II started. By the start of the War, my hometown was only in its first one and a half-decade of existence. Panganiban used to be a part of its neighboring municipality, Viga, Catanduanes, until it was finally declared a separate entity in 1921. It was first named Payo, covering a 7,772 km^2 area of valleys, plains, and hills. Panganiban is bounded by the municipalities of Bagamanoc, Viga, and Caramoran in its northern, southern, and western borders, respectively. The boundary between Caramoran and Panganiban was covered with dense forest. On the other side, my hometown's eastern side faces the Pacific Ocean. Panganiban is fifty-six kilometers away from Virac, the capital of Catanduanes. Back in the 1940s to 1950s, the population in the municipality was just a couple of thousands. Now, it is just a few steps away from ten thousand! But one thing I am really proud of, from then until now, Panganibanons know each other.

Panganiban is rich in natural and living resources, too. The vast valleys support the local rice production in Panganiban. During the planting season, farmers would wake up early, prepare and bring their equipment and carabaos, and start plowing their fields in preparation for planting. They had to start early so that they were already finished with their work by the time the sun was already at its peak. Then, after some days, the farmers would start sowing *palay*, the local name for rice. Since then until now, these vast rice fields create scenery that is comparable to a sea of green. After planting, farmers would wait until their *palay* becomes ready for harvest. It usually takes five to six months. The harvest season was evident even to the young kids like us because it turned the rice fields into shimmering gold.

But Panganiban offers more. Its hills are also filled with native abaca and coconut. In appearance, abaca closely resembles a banana tree, only that its fruits cannot be eaten, and its body is used in cloth production. During my childhood, the abaca in Panganiban clothe us when other types of textiles and fabrics were unavailable for us. Even though abaca is now planted in other parts of the world, it actually originated in the Philippines. And proud enough, Catanduanes is the top abaca producer in the country.

The case for the coconuts is not that different at all. The Philippines is also known as an exporter of coconuts and its products, and Catanduanes and Panganiban, of course, have a share of it. Every part of the coconut has its own use, giving it its name "the tree of life." From food to shelter, coconuts served the local people of Panganiban very well. That was very important during the days of the War because of the limited supply of goods. And even for me as a child, these trees have shared plenty of fun and unforgettable experiences.

The coasts of Panganiban are something to be proud of, too. Lining them are thick mangroves, mitigating the dancing waves coming from the Pacific Ocean. Catanduanes's unfortunate location makes it the very first Philippine landmass to be battered by typhoons that originate from the Pacific. As part of the "Land of the Howling Winds," Panganiban is no stranger to the damages often brought by such typhoons. Back in my childhood, these coastlines weren't that familiar as I live far from the shores.

Among my hometown's natural resources, coal deposits were something that I was very familiar with. It was during the War when the Japanese tapped on these resources and made my hometown a hotspot for the troops. As a child, it was an enjoyment more than terror. I was innocent enough to understand what those coals were used for, nor why were the Japanese soldiers so committed to utilizing them. I am going to reserve the story about the coal deposits for the later chapter.

In the mid to late 20th century, the livelihood in Panganiban was simple. We did not have gadgets like today, and all we had were everything offered by nature. As I can recall, most people I knew were involved in farms or dressmaking. As a boy, I had a firsthand experience of being a farm boy. No, it wasn't an experience because it was, in fact, my life during those times. Boys were trained to do farm activities because we were expected to take over the farms when we grow up. On the other hand, most ladies were involved in dressmaking. I remember my sisters and mother making clothes for the family. They also attend to household chores such as cleaning the house and doing the laundry.

Having witnessed the progress and development of Panganiban, I must say thatso many things have already changed. But nonetheless, the same Panganiban that I knew would remain inscribed in my heart and memory. Less than a quarter of a century of my life happened in Panganiban, my beloved hometown. It had witnessed the hardships that I inevitably was born to. It witnessed World War II that had been a huge part of my childhood. Nevertheless, it also witnessed how I outgrew the War and how I have turned from the little boy who used to buy candies from the Japanese to the successful Frank that I am now.

CHAPTER 2

THE DE LA ROSA FAMILY

The family structure in the Philippines is relatively more complex than that of the other nations. Filipinos are known for having large extended families that include several generations. We have the words *apo sa tuhod*, which refers to the children of our grandchildren. We have our *lolo and lola sa tuhod* or the parents of our grandmothers and grandfathers. We treat our second cousins as no different from our first cousins. In fact, if you are persistent enough, you may even link everyone in a community as family members in a genealogy!

In the Philippines, these connections are not simply used in a family pedigree. A typical Filipino household consists of the main family and a few members from their extended families. These are usually the grandparents and grandchildren. And by saying these things, I do not mean that it is a bad thing. In fact, I must say that the family structure in the Philippines makes a household livelier and fun.

Nanay and *tatay* are the respective Tagalog words for mother and father. Back when I was a child, most children call their parents as such. We also have several variations, such as *inang, inay, ina, tatang, and ama.* Personally, my siblings and I call our parents Nanay and Tatay. Those words are very dear to me because they remind me of my childhood, my carefree days together with my parents in Panganiban.

Nanay's maiden name was Anatalia Villegas Aguilar, while Tatay's full name was Eulogio Vega De La Rosa. They were from the second generation of our family tree in Panganiban. Nanay and Tatay were almost the same age, with less than a year difference. They were married in the early twentieth century when life was even simpler than it was during my childhood. According to my parents, they grew up doing everything the hard way. As a customary responsibility among women of her time, my Nanay did her laundry either in the flowing water of the nearby rivers or with the water from a dug-up well in their backyard. There was no water supply back then so, they also bathe and collect water for household use from these sources. After washing the clothes, Nanay had to bleach and dry the laundry through the scorching heat of the sun. Once dried, the next step was to iron the clothes, but not with the flat iron that we know nowadays. The flat iron during those times was heavier and more complicated. It required burning charcoal to heat the clothes. These charcoals were made from hardwood or coconut shells, whichever material was available. Tatay had the opportunity to attend primary education until the fourth grade, but Nanay wasn't given the same chance. During their youth, there was still a huge discrepancy between men's and women's right to education. Furthermore, women back then were expected to simply attend to the household chores and domestic needs of the family. Thinking about it now, I am still confused about whether their lives were simpler or harder.

I am not certain whether this was the same case in other countries, but back in history, most Filipinos marry at a young age. Arranged marriages were still common, and most young ladies were married off by their parents even before they reached their twenties. Nonetheless, that was not the case for my parents. It was in their late twenties when Nanay and Tatay were wedded. Before the Japanese occupation, the Philippines was colonized by Spain for more than three hundred years. As a result, Roman Catholicism became the most dominant religion in our country. My parent's wedding ceremony was held in a Catholic church, and as such, was headed by a priest.

We have had a very happy family despite the contrast of the on-going War. The fruit of my parent's love for each other was eight children, named Luz, Gloria, Antonio, Jose, Francisco, Pedro, Maria, and Dionisia, arranged according to birth. Back in those times, large families were very common. In fact, it was very rare for families to have children of less than five. Having a large family was a good thing back then, though it may still be the case until now. But during those times, many children meant many helping hands to assist the fathers on the farm and the mothers in their household chores. More than that, I consider our big family as a blessing because having each other's company made our lives lighter and happier, especially because we were very close to one another. We did things together. We worked together, ate together, and went to church together. There was never a task too difficult because our family always worked as a team. In our small wooden house, the ten of us lived in abundance and joy despite the on-going War around us!

Respect was the main theme in every Filipino family, and ours was not an exemption. From a very young age, every child I knew was trained to address their elders respectfully. We used the words *po* and *opo,* which signify our respect for people older than us. I believe only Filipinos have such words, which onlyshows how valuable respect is in our culture. As a child, I deeply understood its importance and was determined to cautiously practice respectful gestures. Aside from saying *po* and *opo*, my siblings and I also kissed my parents' and otherelders' hands. For us, it wasn't a task; it was just part of who we were as children. Aside from respect, there were lots of other things that we learned from our parents. They may be lacking in terms of educational background, but I must say that my parents were very rich in terms of family values. Nanay and Tatay taught us the importance of honesty, love for oneself and one's fellowmen, and being appreciative of everything we do and have because they were all blessings from God. My parents gave me the right character to see things positively and bestowed me with the attitude and perseverance to seek success.

Chapter 3

The Little Frank was Born

I was born in the year 1937, which I, of course, consider special. It was two years after Manuel Quezon was named as the second president of the Philippines and the first president of the Commonwealth. Internationally, it was Adolf Hitler's fourth year as a leader of Germany. During that time, Hitler was already fueling the upcoming World War II just a couple of years away. In Great Britain, Prime Minister Neville Chamberlain had just been appointed to the position, the first British Prime Minister to face Hitler before and during the onset of the War. He was the predecessor of Winston Churchill.

My birth was not special. I was not an important person back then. I didn't come from a prominent family of any public figure. Nevertheless, I consider my birth as a special gift from God, and I believe my family would also agree. Every member of our family was a blessing, and I doubt if things would have turned out the same, even if only one of us was missing.

It was on the fifth of June, the year 1937. I was born in a small wooden house located under the shady blackberry tree in a very small and remote village in Panganiban. According to Nanay, I was delivered by a midwife, which we locally call *partera*. Back then, there were only a few hospitals in the country and less to none on a remote island like ours. Most Filipinos were still in poverty, and the chance of studying medicine was often limited to wealthy families. As a result, most children were born in their own homes, through the assistance of the *partera.* In fact, home birth was normal during those times. Even before the Philippines was colonized, this had been practiced in almost every part of the country. Tribes and communities had their own birth attendants, and depending on their culture, they also had their set of birthing rituals.

Unlike hospital doctors, a *partera* does not have formal education nor any formal training in child delivery. They are often the elderlies in the community, and probably, they have attended and watched numerous deliveries already that they learned how to do it themselves. They may have learned through experience, and that isn't a bad thing at all. In times when formal education was still limited, the experience was the best teacher for us. That is true not just for the *partera*, but also for other professions as well. For example, even at a young age, I was already knowledgeable in farming even though I didn't have any background in agricultural studies yet. Everything I knew was from the guidance of Tatay and my elder brothers, as well as from my personal experiences.

It was the morning of June 5th. After going through pain and giving out her cries, Nanay successfully gave birth to her fifth child. Nanay and Tatay decided to name the child Francisco, with my nickname, Frank. The little Frank was the fifth child and the third son of the family. Back in 1937, the fate that awaited me as a little Frank was still unknown, but despite that, I still grew up as a happy, contented, and well- loved child! From 1937, my story started in our small community in Panganiban, before, during, and after the Second World War.

I was not born into a wealthy family. No, I was actually born to a poor one. My first home was a wooden house made from the hard woods of narra tree, a material that was abundant locally during those times. We actually had two wooden houses, one in town proper and one in Camonohan at the foot of the mountain where we hid from the Japanese during the war; the same house where I was born under the blackberry tree. Poverty was no stranger to me; it was a friend instead. Like other families in town, my family had no access to electricity. Our food supply relied on Tatay's farm produce. Money was scarce. Despite these circumstances, I still consider my early life as a beautiful one. From 1937 to this day, I consider myself blessed beyond expectations.

CHAPTER 4

THE SECOND WORLD WAR

The twentieth century had been a century of wars. It witnessed millions of people losing their lives. Millions of houses burning down to ashes. Years' worth of livelihood being perished. Millions of children died, and if not, they became orphans.

Before there was a Second World War, there has to be the first. Just three decades earlier, World War I, also known as the Great War, took place. It was a war between the Central Powers, including Germany, Turkey, and Austria-Hungary, and the Allies, including France, Russia, Great Britain, Italy, and Japan. Unlike in the second world war, the Southeast Asian nations were indirectly involved, not unless they were a colony of the participating nations.

Among the neighboring countries of the Philippines, Japan, China, Vietnam, and Thailand (known as Siam) were the most affected and involved. Japan, China, and Thailand opted to join the War to advance their political interests during the time. They were fighting for their territories, for power. However, Vietnam was different. Like the Philippines, it had been long colonized by the European forces. Specifically, Vietnam was controlled by the

French, which was a main participant of the War. The French enticed the poverty-stricken Vietnamese to provide armed forces in return for an attractive wage. Most Vietnamese were farmers too, and understanding the economic challenges of the time, it was not difficult to comprehend why they risked their lives for causes that weren't theirs.

The U.S. remained neutral in the first three years of the War; however, it finally decided to take the side of the Allies in 1917. During those times, the Philippines was "owned" by the U.S. because they bought us from Spain. As a result, Filipinos built submarines and a ship to aid the U.S. troops. We sent 25,000 soldiers and helped detain German crews and confiscate their ships. The Pacific wasn't the stage of the Great War, so our damages were limited to the deaths and casualties.

Though there was no way I could have known it as a child, looking at the history now made me realize that World War II wouldn't happen if not for the Great War. The Great War brought significant impacts in terms of territories and political powers. Many nation-states were established, and many empires collapsed. It encouraged European nations to demand their independence. It helped the U.S. become a world power. But most importantly, it fueled communism in the Soviet Union and led to the rise of Hitler to power in Germany.

World War II formally started in September 1939, just two years after my birth. Later in my life, I learned that it actually started with Germany's aggression toward neighboring nations for the ultimate goal of expanding Germany's territory. When Hitler invaded Poland, Great Britain and France resorted to declaring war. Soon enough, almost all European nations were at war.

But WWII in Europe was another thing for us. Closer to home, in the Pacific, Japan was declaring war in support of and with the same goal as Germany. WWII reached the Philippines in 1941 when the Japanese launched a surprise aerial attack shortly after the infamous Pearl Harbor bombing. It was followed by a series of Japanese soldier landings both in the north and south of Manila.

The Philippines was still under the Americans during this period, and the military was headed by Gen. Douglas McArthur. Army units composed of Filipino and American soldiers were established, but they were soon defeated due to a lack of support and supply coming in for them. These soldiers were imprisoned and were subjected to the ill-reputed Bataan Death March that we'd soon heard of in Panganiban. The U.S. was caught off guard, which led to the temporary victory of the Japanese in the country. Soldiers infiltrated every island of the Philippines, and there, they did their atrocities. This is also where our terrors began.

Before the start of the Second World War, I have to admit that our community was already in poverty. However, the onset of the War and its coming to the country made our situation even worse. When the Japanese started to occupy the country, Catanduanes was not given an exemption. In my hometown came these Japanese soldiers in their uniforms, carrying firearms with them all the time. Having heard of the Manila Bombings and the Bataan Death March, the very presence of these foreign soldiers sent chills to our spines. Everyone in our community was so afraid that we decided to move and hide at the foot of the nearby mountain.

Staying in a place where the Japanese were also present meant giving up everything that we had. From the moment they arrived, they already owned all of our possessions. At any time, they can go from house to house, collecting any property or asset that they would like. They can take our pigs, chickens, and any other livestock. They can pick any fruits in our garden, even the foods that were already served on our tables. No one dared question the Japanese soldiers because doing so was synonymous with requesting physical abuse or death!

To at least give ourselves some form of protection, we moved from Panganiban town proper to Camonohan, where my parents owned a farm. We decided to stay in the same wooden house where I was born, under the same shade of the blackberry tree. Our parcel of land was planted with coconut trees. Around us were other kinds of crops planted by our neighbors from town. Out of fear, they also hid along the foot of the mountain in Camonohan. They built new huts there and took out lands to produce their foods. They cleared these lands by burning the woods in a system called *kaingin.* Once cleared, they started planting all kinds of food crops and raised their livestock in the background. We did not consider these crops and livestock as ours because we knew that anytime that a Japanese took an interest in them, they could easily take them away from us.

Camonohan was the place at the foot of the mountain. The trees of the mountain offered protection to its new inhabitants. They made us less visible to the eyes of the Japanese; thus, we were less likely to get hurt or, worse, be killed. Near our new settlement was a road leading to the town. That was the road that we usually take whenever we needed to go to the town proper.

The fear that the Japanese occupation instilled in the locals was so serious that there was this specific story going around. This story was so popular back then that I can still recall it despite my young age during the time. According to the story, there was a farmer living on the other side of the mountain where we were living. This farmer was so scared and anxious that the Japanese soldiers would kill him and take his farm produce and livestock. So, the farmer thought of a way to keep the soldiers away from his land.

Up in the mountain, there was this wild variant of yam called *namo.* In times of scarcity, *namo* can be eaten by the locals who know how to properly prepare them. However, the wild yam becomes poisonous if not sufficiently cooked. So early in the morning, the farmer went up the mountain to collect tons of *namo.* Then, down to his hut, he loaded the yams in a big pot placed over the fire. When the yam started cooking, the farmer went back up to the mountain to hide. As the farmer approached his hut later on the same day, everything was quiet. There was no Japanese walking around. Instead, they were lying on the ground. At first, the farmer thought that the Japanese were just tired and decided to sleep around his hut. So, the farmer looked for a tree and climbed up of it. There, he had a better view of the scenery in front of his eyes. There were more Japanese on the ground than he initially thought. Indeed, the hungry Japanese took his bait and ate all the *namo* that he left in his big pot.

Having lived during the horrible times of WWII, I cannot blame the farmer for committing such an act. The fear that we had, especially for the adults who understood very well what was going around, could make us do what we otherwise thought was impossible. We can flee anytime if need be. We can stay hidden in the shades and shadows of a tree just to be invisible even for a while. When pushed to limitations, it was not impossible for our fears to be turned into something horrible yet somehow reasonable. Not that I support the killings; I just understood where the farmer was coming from. Everyone in our neighborhood did understand, too.

On a national scale, Filipinos showed bravery and determination to win back their independence and fight against the atrocities that we were subjected to. After the defeat of the army unit created to fight against the Japanese, many underground groups and guerillas were formed. The *Hukbo ng Bayan Laban sa Japan* (HUKBALAHAP), or the "People's Anti-Japanese Army" in English, fought against the puppet government formed by the Japanese in the Philippines. After the Japanese victory, many elites in the country supported them for several reasons as they claimed—to protect their families, their interests, and their belief that it would be better for us to be in ally with another Asian country.

But the members of the HUKBALAHAP and other guerillas believed otherwise. They fought for independence and independence alone. They denounced and rejected the murders, rapes, massacres, and other crimes being committed by the Japanese all over the country. They also targeted the elites who joined forces with their enemies. The groups were composed of insurgents and even escapees of the Bataan Death March. Interestingly, they were able to recruit a significant number of members. They fought against the Japanese government even after the end of WWII. They fought for the peasants and the farmers, a cause that was very important for typical Filipino families like ours.

CHAPTER 5

WWII IN PANGANIBAN

What I have mentioned so far are the atrocities that were experienced by many during WWII. These are the general experiences of the people who were subjected to injustices during that dark period of history. In fact, there is no need to emphasize how difficult our lives were back then. Anyone who has lived during any war would have known the social and economic setbacks of such events. The same thing was true in Panganiban, and all the people living in this town.

My family was in deep poverty when I was growing up. Aside from the resources available in nature, almost everything I could think of now was scarce. We had no money. Even food, a basic necessity for survival, was very difficult to acquire. We relied on our farms to support our food requirements, and our neighborhood depended on one another to help each and every one survives. I must say that without the rich and available land of Panganiban, many of us wouldn't have made it this far. Of course, the hard-working and resilient nature of Filipinos also helped us survive such difficulties of the time.

Rice is a staple food in the Philippines. Filipinos eat rice three times a day—for breakfast, lunch, and dinner. Ask a typical Filipino, and more likely than not, they wouldn't survive a day without rice. Luckily, Panganiban was and still is, rich in farmlands. Its valleys and plains offer Panganibanons a reliable source of rice to feed the town's population. The same situation was also true during my childhood. Most fathers and boys in the family were trained to work on the farm and plant food crops to feed the family.

As a child, I can still remember how we used to eat rice sprinkled with salt on top. Viand was a luxury back then, and having meat on the table was very rare. On occasions when even rice was unavailable, we had no choice but to collect sweet potatoes and other root crops from our farm. To add flavor to the meal, we usually prepare finely chopped coconut meat and put it on top of the sweet potatoes. For our drinking water, there were two options available back then. We can either fetch water from a shallow, dug-up well or dig a spring alongside the nearby riverbank. Our situation got even worse whenever typhoons visited Panganiban. Situated close to the Pacific, the wind was really strong that very few to no crops could remain standing during the storms' onslaught. Our crops would die that our only options would be to collect fallen fruits and produce on the ground. Often, rivers were flooded with muddy water after the typhoon passed, so our drinking water was also compromised. Thinking of it now made me realize how nature played a role in making our lives easier and sometimes harder too.

Compared to food, money was even more scarce in Panganiban. Almost every person I knew was considered poor to very poor, and

I doubt if any of them have had more than enough money during WWII. As far as I can remember, everyone in Panganiban was living with the bare minimum, juggling whatever resources were available just to survive. We had no electricity during that time. Our only light sources were the gas lamps made from cans, clothes, bottles or any materials that one can make of. We had no television or radio, and the only mode of communication was through word of mouth. Whenever there was an important announcement to be made, the town crier, which usually was a policeman, would go to a corner of the town. Blowing his whistle, the folks living around that corner would gather to listen for the announcement. Then, the town crier would move to the next corner, doing the same methods all over again until every person in town has had received the important message. There was no public transportation, either. Lucky for us, we had draft animals such as carabaos that helped transport ourselves and other heavy equipment. When I was still a child, long-distance walking was still normal, and it was expected from everyone; thus, the lack of other forms of transportation was not big of an issue back then. We can walk from the town to the foot of the mountain. We can walk back and forth multiple times a day if necessary. Even we as students walked to our schools barefooted. Imagining it would be difficult for the younger generations, but during our time, we never had any complaints. Being able to attend school was more than enough reason to be thankful!

Our little community was composed of households that I classified into two—the nipa hut and the non-nipa hut households. For the longest time, nipa hut, locally called *bahay kubo,* has been a national symbol of the Philippines. It is made of local materials, including bamboo, palm, rattan, and vines. Building a nipa hut does not require any sophisticated equipment. In fact, men and women in a neighborhood can easily build one as long as there are enough materials. The sides of the *bahay kubo* are often made of bamboos tied together to create a solid wall. To make the hut's thatched roof, nipa shingles are tied to the central bamboo stick called *powdan*. The nipa shingles are made from green nipa leaves collected from *sasa,* a palm variety that grows in places where water is available—near the swamp or anywhere alongside the coastline of every town and village. Coconut palms can also be used for this purpose. Then, once the shingles are ready, they are tied to the *rafters* using dried vines or rattan, which act as the rope.

Bahay kubo has been home to native Filipinos even before the Spaniards came to colonize us. It has been home to countless generations of families, and in no doubt symbolizes Filipino resilience and the simplicity of life in the country. It has made a significant contribution to Filipino culture and tradition. But as the country developed, *bahay kubo* slowly became a symbol of poverty among the people. Filipinos who have the resources to build stronger houses shift to wooden, and later on, concrete homes. The families who lack the money or even the materials are left living in their *bahay kubo* that are susceptible to damages, especially during the typhoon season.

When I was growing up, there were still lots of nipa huts in our community. My family was fortunate to have owned a wooden house at that time. It was probably because of my parents' hard work and the abundance of trees in our farmlands. However, my friends and classmates were not as fortunate as I was. Back then, most of them were still living in their *bahay kubo,* and as such, other villagers considered them the poorest. But that was not true for me; I saw things differently. For me, the families living in *bahay kubo* were the happiest families in Panganiban. Their lives were simple and plain, and I considered them as the happiest people in the world. They had fewer worries; and, thus, were able to enjoy life's simplicity. Compared to other families, they had fewer properties and assets, but because they believe that the merciful God would always take good care of them, they never let their poverty take control of their lives. Instead, they supported their needs by planting staple crops such as beans, corn, and bananas. They also took care of chickens and let them run around their huts. For me, those people were the wealthiest in the village because they lived in an abundance of love, joy, and peace. As for me, I spent most of my childhood years in our wooden house at the foot of the mountain. Though we were not living in a *bahay kubo,* I still considered my family as also one of the happiest in our neighborhood. Our household was filled with love and affection from our dear parents.

Our wooden house was standing in Santo Santiago street in Ilaya, Panganiban. We had no house number because, with the small population of the municipality, the mailman knew everyone in town! Every street of Panganiban, in Ilaya and Ilawod, led to the central town where St. James the Greater Parish Church is located. The church was named in honor of Panganiban's patron saint, St. James, the greater. During those times, our church was central to almost all the activities in town. This is quite understandable because after being colonized by the Spaniards for more than three centuries, every Filipino family and community put God and the church in their core values. Prior to WWII, Panganiban also had a primary school for children. We had no secondary school yet, which made completing high school more challenging. One had to walk to another town just to complete their secondary levels. However, during WWII, all the schools were closed. And I think even if they weren't close, very few to no children could have afforded to attend classes for economic and safety reasons.

These streets and institutions were familiar to everyone in Panganiban, but they would never be as familiar to the homeless people in town. As a child, I got to know two homeless individuals living with us in Panganiban. By the time I met them, I was so innocent that I was still unaware of how they were living their lives. One time, when my family was having dinner, I was surprised to see an unfamiliar face seated with us at the table. My parents were hospitable people, and it was normal for us to warmly welcome people to share meals with us. But what was odd was that the lady was unfamiliar, and I had not seen her in our neighborhood before. She was an old, wrinkled woman with gray hair and was around the age of sixty at the time. The unfamiliar woman was carrying a black bag, which I presumed contained her belongings. As a curious child, I intently observed the appearance of the old lady and watched her take her meal as she used our utensils and ate the same food as ours.

During the dinner, I couldn't ask my parents who the woman was because it would be rude and disrespectful. Every Filipino child was taught to be respectful to everyone, especially to the elders. So, it was only after dinner that I had the opportunity to ask my mother who our visitor was. Only then did I learn that the lady was called Tiya Biyay by the townspeople. She had no home nor family. In order to survive, Tiya Biyay went from house to house to beg for food. At times, she cooked her own foods and kept them for days as her meal. When she was available, she also helped us worked in our garden and farms. Tiya Biyay stayed in our house for a few more days, and since then, she became close to the people in our neighborhood. The story of Tiya Biyay broke my heart as a child, but in my old age now, I realized that despite her sad story, God had blessed her with a long life.

There was another homeless person whom I met during my childhood. He was called Toto by the villagers, by the adults and children alike. Like Tiya Biyay, he also had no home, no wife, and no children. He was sixty-two years old back then, with an all-wrinkled and unshaven face. Toto was known by everyone in town who also helped him survive the difficulties of life. Whenever there were social gatherings, events, or celebrations in Panganiban, Toto was always present but not as a guest. He always worked behind the scene, helping the celebrants prepare for the event, cook the foods, wash the dishes, throw the garbage, and such. In return, he would be fed in the kitchen. When there were foods left after every guest had gone home, he would receive packed foods that would last for at least a few meals. Even those small acts of kindness were a blessing for him. Because he was homeless, Toto used to keep his packed foods under the bushes near the place where he slept. But the kids in the town were clueless about the repercussions of their actions. To have fun, the children used to sneak to Toto's bushes and steal his food. It was a game for the children, but for Toto, it meant another missed meal. So, after some time, Toto finally learned his lesson and brought his packed meals wherever he went.

Without a doubt, WWII caused unimaginable difficulties among the townspeople. Nonetheless, the camaraderie and unity that was present in Panganiban made such challenges a whole lot more manageable. Even though everyone was in poverty, I can proudly say that none of us were selfish enough not to share anything we had with those who were in need. In the end, friendship still matters more than wealth!

CHAPTER 6

THE SECOND WORLD WAR FOR THE YOUNG FRANK

WWII was a very dark time for almost everyone. It stalled the developments that followed the Great War and caused another set of economic, social, and political problems. In whatever aspects of life you look at, WWII was never beneficial. But for the innocent eyes, there was still a good side to their sufferings.

As a child, I knew that the Japanese were not our friends. My parents and all elders in the village were afraid of them. They abused anyone that stood against them. They took anything that they wanted. It was the truth back then, we were poor, and we were being taken advantage of by the foreigners. But for the children like myself, this tragic situation still offered something to enjoy.

Life is more complicated nowadays because back then, the lives of every child in Panganiban were almost all alike. The typical kids in town belonged to a poor family. They lived in either wooden houses or nipa huts just to protect them from external elements such as rain and wind. They have two loving parents, their

Nanay and Tatay, and siblings who were rarely less than five in number. Large families were normal; in fact, I must say that the bigger the family, the happier they were. Interestingly, the bigger household size did not make the family members distant from one another. Every family in my hometown was tightly knit, doing household and farm works together. They also worshipped and attended church services with one another.

Like today, every child in Panganiban had the need for love, nurture, and affection. Proudly enough, every family in town was also able to meet these needs despite the chaos that was going around. Every parent I knew was loving to their children. They took care of their children even if it would take time to attend to the children's needs one by one. The typical kids back then also had the unending curiosity to see and understand the world around them. Unlike today, we did not have the luxury of the internet to research any questions that we had. We were not able to see beyond our island. The only resources that we had were the things around us and the wisdom passed on by the elders in the community to the younger ones.

I was one of the typical kids in town. I lived in a wooden hut with two loving parents and seven siblings. As a child, I was showered with love and affection, and I have no question about that. Since I was a kid, I have always been thirsty for knowledge, observing everything around me, and seeking answers and explanations whenever and wherever possible. So naturally, I started my inquiry on the things that were happening around our small community.

I couldn't have known it before, but now, I found it unusual that the Japanese were really friendly to children. Even though I had plenty of encounters with them, I know for a fact that I never experienced any form of harassment or abuse. The same thing was true for other children in our neighborhood. Probably, the Japanese were just fond of kids. But regardless of whatever reason, I am thankful because it made the dark days of WWII tolerable for the young minds and souls in Panganiban. In fact, because of their friendliness to us, children, I even had fun and exciting memories with them. Maybe because that was the only life available for us back then that our playful and innocent nature made us turn the hardships into a positive experience. For us, the kids in Panganiban, meeting the Japanese was more fun than scary.

There is no need to say how money was so scarce back in the days of WWII. Our families were very poor, and we didn't experience having more than what we needed to survive. But back in the mid-'90s, what is considered a small amount now could already afford us so much. U.S. has had the highest GDP from 1940, but despite being a colony of Uncle Sam, the Philippine currency remained of a lesser value.

When the Japanese came to Panganiban, they established a garrison out of a building previously owned by our former town mayor. It was a big store that was running perfectly well before the Japanese came into the picture. However, when the foreign soldiers started to infiltrate the town, our town mayor fled somewhere else and started a new life there. The vacated building was left unused, which the Japanese took possession of. The building acted as their headquarter in Panganiban, and thus, was always filled with uniformed soldiers. As kids, we were so attracted to the garrison but not because of the building nor by the soldiers. Instead, we loved the place because of the candies! The Japanese revived the store and sold candies and all other small stuff for kids. Children did not have the opportunity to hold a huge amount of money in their hands, but a single cent already meant a lot. In fact, the kids who kept a cent in their pockets were already considered rich by their playmates. The store in the garrison sold lemon drops, a candy that was a favorite of every child in Panganiban. And for us, one cent was already a luxury because it could already buy us a lot of lemon drops! Lemon drops were so special to us that if one had many and the other one had none, the latter would befriend the former just so he or she would be given a lemon drop as a peace offering. That was one of the get around when we did not have a cent in the pocket.

Unfortunately, not all kids had one cent. Some kids were from a really poor household whose parents could not afford to give them one. Sometimes, even our parents did not have extra coins to give us. The money that they had was only enough to buy food and other needs for the house. And so our resourceful minds were put into action. Instead of waiting for the grace to befall us, we worked to earn the grace instead. So, if the kids did not have a cent in their pocket, they would find a household that was in need of help in doing the household chores. Basically, the children in Panganiban offered their services in exchange for a cent! After doing a day of menial household tasks, each child would receive one cent for their hard work. I cannot express our happiness whenever a cent touched our palms!

Among my most memorable experiences with the Japanese were the trips to the coal mine. When I grew up and had the opportunity to understand the real causes of WWII, especially in the Pacific, I learned that one of the reasons why the Japanese attacked several territories was to find natural sources of energy. Their supply was cut by the U.S., and their only chance of being a world power relied on their ability to power their warships and their other industrial operations. I believe it was for this reason that the Japanese took notice of our small town. Panganiban was rich in natural resources, including coal. About eighteen kilometers from the garrison, there was a spot in the mountain where the Japanese used to mine coals. Every day, a truck would go up to the mountain, collect coal, deliver it to the port to fire and heat their steamboats and go back to the garrison. Japanese soldiers were really friendly to us, kids. They sometimes would give us candies and small stuff to play with. On other occasions, they would invite us to join them in picking up and delivering the coal. The ride going up and down the mountain was our favorite. Because of the rocky road and the changing terrain, it was like a roller- coaster ride for us children. We enjoyed riding their huge truck and going around the mountain and the town while on it. Back then, it was all fun and adventure, but now, I already know that those Japanese took advantage of the natural resources available in my beloved hometown.

Earlier, I had mentioned that when the Japanese arrived in Panganiban, everyone was in a panic that we all flew from the town to the foot of the mountain in Camonohan. It was our initial reaction out of fear. But as the situation settled and we somehow got used to our new lives with the Japanese, little by little, we mustered the courage to occasionally go back to the town for important activities.

Our wooden house in town remained standing even though it was often empty. To keep ourselves safe, we opted to live in the house near our farms. But during special occasions, we also stayed in town to attend activities such as church services. We used to walk from Camonohan to the town, leaving our crops and livestock for a short time. When in town, we knew that the Japanese would not harm us as long as we follow them and abide by their rules. We had to bow our heads whenever we passed by their headquarters to pay respect. I can still remember how we used to greet them with the unknown foreign words *gumbawa, ohayo, or konitsiwa.* There was no way we could have understood what the words meant. Even now, I do not know the correct spellings; I just wrote them the way they were spoken. I think the three words translate to good evening, good day, or good afternoon, but I am still unsure, though.

Bowing was, and always is, an important part of the Japanese culture. It is used on many occasions and signifies different things depending on the circumstances. One may bow as a form of respect, as a sign of guilt, or even to plead for his or her life. In our case in Panganiban, I could say that the Japanese soldiers expected us to bow as a sign of respect to them because of their higher social status back then. In Japan, there are also different types of bows. Based on my understanding, it is a rule of thumb to bow lower when you have lower social status than the other person. The higher the gap in your societal positions, the higher the gap in your bows too.

Even though the aggressive occupants of our town dictated and affected most of our everyday activities, there was still something in us that remained unique. Thinking about it, I have to say that the Filipino culture is really rich. Before the Spaniards came, we already had our own form of life. We had our own form of writing. Each community followed its own form of government. In the pre-colonial Philippines, education, as we know it today, was still non-existent. And as such, medicine was practiced in traditional and non-scientific ways.

During WWII, hospitals and trained medical doctors were very rare. Aside from those who belonged to wealthy families, most Filipinos could not afford to complete tertiary education, more so attend a medical school. As an island province, we were also in isolation from the main islands of the Philippines, making it harder for both public and private hospitals to provide the needed medical services. And even if they were present, very few, if not none, could and would have afforded the services because of the lack of extra money. The good thing was that despite the scientific advancements since the pre-colonial period, the traditional medicinal practice still survived. The knowledge and techniques were transferred from one generation to another, and I believe that there is still some practicing it even today.

One time when I was around twelve to thirteen years old, I was visited by an unknown disease. I felt really sick that I could not eat anything. I became so skinny, and my mother was really worried. She tried every home remedy that she knew of, but none worked at all. Back then, I don't think there were any hospitals or clinics around the town. Nonetheless, I am sure that even if there was one, my family could not afford to pay for the fees and medicine. And so, my family had no choice but to call the *arbularyo.* In the Filipino culture, *arbularyo* are quack doctors who practice medicine using herbs or any plant parts such as bark, leaves, fruits, roots, and even seeds. The term *arbularyo* itself was an ancient word for the herbalist. I do not know the case today, but back then, *arbularyo* was considered really effective. They were the first to be called whenever someone was sick or an unknown ailment was felt by the townspeople. They used plants and other herbs available in the community to do their medicinal practices.

One of our neighbors, Nang Goling, was knowledgeable about the practices performed by *arbularyo.* Out of her desperate situation, Nanay asked Nang Goling to come to our home and take a look at my condition. So one morning, Nang Goling came to our home and gathered all kinds of leaves from our garden. Our house was surrounded by all kinds of tropical fruits—citrus, guava, soursop, and many more, which I cannot recall anymore. Nang Goling picked the young leaves from all the fruit trees in our backyard and later on mixed them all together. Then, she heated the leaves over our wooden stove. When all the leaves were sufficiently heated, she spread them over my body and covered me with a cloth. I can still remember the warmth that flowed through my body. The moist and tender texture of the leaves gave me a relaxing and comforting feeling, something that I did not get to feel since I got sick.

After what Nang Goling did, I started to feel energized once again. I was able to feel alive again after a seemingly long time. Interestingly, only then was I able to realize my hunger after not eating any meal for the past few days. So, upon feeling the emptiness of my stomach, my loving mother hurriedly went to the kitchen to prepare *lugaw. Lugaw,* or porridge in English, was the favorite food of sick people, especially the children. It was prepared by boiling rice in water and adding salt and pepper to taste. Some may add ginger too. If available, using chicken broth and chicken meat was better, of course! *Lugaw* was the perfect food for the sick because it is soft and tender, which eliminates the need for chewing. As we all know, being sick is energy-draining to the point that we cannot even chew our own foods. *Lugaw* also has a plain taste, which may be advantageous or disadvantageous depending on one's condition. As for me, my mother knew very well how to make me get up to eat my *lugaw.* She would fry dried fish, which we called *sapsap,* and put it on top of my food. Then, she will squeeze some calamondin, small citrus fruits that are common in the Philippines. The soft texture of *lugaw*, the salty taste of *sapsap,* and the sour juices of calamondin was the perfect meal combination to regain my energy back! After being treated and after eating my mother's specially prepared lugaw, I got back my lost energy and was able to play once again. Thanks to Nang Goling and to the trees in our backyard, I was able to overcome my illness. Despite her limited knowledge and training of being an *arbularyo,* Nang Goling still saved me from my physical pain.

But that was not the only time I got sick. One summer in a few years after the incident, I got sick once again. I was in Napo, herding the carabaos in our farm. While doing the task, I knew that I was not feeling well, and I had to get back home as soon as possible. So, I took the herd back to the barn in our backyard and quickly went upstairs. Upon seeing my face, Nanay noticed right away that I was sick. I started throwing up, which made my mother panic even more. She ran downstairs to call our good neighbor, Nang Goling, but unfortunately, she wasn't home that time. There was no one in the neighborhood who was knowledgeable in treating ailments, so Nanay asked my elder sister, Luz, to go see our Uncle Policarpio and to tell him that I was seriously sick. She further instructed my sister to ask Uncle Policarpio to immediately send an *arbularyo* to our home.

Upon hearing the situation, Uncle Policarpio immediately searched for an *arbularyo* in town. He walked from every side and corner, but he wasn't able to find one. So out of urgency, uncle decided to go and search in the neighboring town. We had no telephone or any form of vehicle back then, so the only option was to walk on foot, from house to house, until he could find someone to help us out. After persistent searching, he was lucky to find one *arbularyo*, an old man around the age of mid-fifty. Uncle Policarpio and the *arbularyo* walked around four kilometers to get to our house. Upon arrival, he put down his black bag, where he had his herbal medications. Inside, there were varieties of dried barks, dried leaves, and even the horn of a deer. He got a bit of everything, mixed them all together, and turned them into powder using mortar and pestle. Then, he added the powder to a glass of drinking water. When dissolved, the old man asked me to drink the resulting solution and explained that by drinking it, I would feel better and well.

I must say that there was nothing ideal about the taste of the drink. It did not taste good, but I knew that if I wanted to get well, I had to do what I was told to. So, I closed my eyes and drunk it all. Afterward, my mother and the rest of the people in the house let me go back to rest. I laid back on the bed, and my mother covered me with a blanket. Before the *arbularyo* came, I had a really high temperature. But after taking in his herbal drink, I immediately started sweating, and I can still remember how my entire body was soaked in perspiration. In the Philippines, sweating is considered a sign of getting well. Scientifically, it is the body's way of cooling down itself.

After everything calmed down, the *arbularyo* told us that, considering my extremely high body temperature, I was lucky to have been saved from a possible convulsion. My mother couldn't thank him and my Uncle Policarpio enough. Without them during that dire moment of my life, I do not know what could have happened instead. Now, if I try to tell this story of mine here in the U.S., most, if not all, would just laugh it out at me. But for my family and me, my personal experiences with the local *arbularyo* were something I will forever be thankful for.

CHAPTER 7

LIVELIHOOD IN PANGANIBAN BEING A VAQUERO

Like most parts of the Philippines in the mid-twentieth century, Panganibanons were predominantly farmers. The municipality's vast plains, hills, and valleys offered more than enough to feed the town's population. Women were mostly housewives, attending to household chores. They took care of the children, cleaned the house and the backyard, and made sure that every family member was healthy and safe. Young ladies were involved in dressmaking, but because of the prevailing poverty, the materials they used were limited to those that were either cheap or were available in nature.

I was a vaquero. Vaquero is a Spanish term that refers to a cowboy or a cattle driver. In the Philippines, the word was adopted to mean a related term, a carabao herder. Carabao is a domesticated water buffalo, around the same size as cattle, and generally covered with black skin. They have black eyes and strong, black horns, which make them look scary at times. Carabaos are found in countries in Southeast Asia. In the Philippines, they were almost everywhere, especially during the twentieth century. They were more common in the provinces where most farms were because they were the farmers' ultimate helper. Carabaos helped us plow the fields. Aside from being a draft animal, they were also sources of milk, meat, and hide. Considering carabaos' vital role in Filipinos' main livelihood in the earlier centuries, there is no question why it was named the country's national animal. Carabaos are rarely seen in metropolitan areas such as in Metro Manila. They are also different from caribou, which most non-Filipino friends think carabaos are related to.

Almost all families in Panganiban owned one or more carabaos. Without them, it was practically impossible to survive. Male carabaos were considered a treasure to every household, including ours, because these animals did all the hard work around the house, on the farm, and in the field. Male carabaos were a necessity in farming. Without the farming technologies that are available today, we had to rely on the strength of our well-loved draft animals. My family owned two males. They helped us in preparing the fields for planting rice, sweet potatoes, and corn. Through plowing and harrowing, the carabaos made the soil loose and friable, perfect for the next cropping season. Our male carabaos were also charged to make furrows. They helped put debris away and improve soil aeration as well. Carabaos are known to be industrious animals, just feed them lots of fresh grasses and give them unlimited drink in the morning, then they are good to go for a whole day of work!

Needless to say, male carabaos are strong. They have powerful muscles and two sickle-shaped horns. One of the most sought-after scenes in the grazeland was the fight between two male carabaos.

The contenders were both big and robust, and who gets to win was always a mystery. Most children in town were fond of watching these beasts fight one another. However, despite the entertainment that the event offered, the children also knew that watching the fight posed a danger. So, to keep ourselves safe, what we often did was to individually find a tree, climb it up, and watch the beasts fight for their lives. When male carabaos fight, they literally fight for their lives. Using their long, sharp horns, they pierce their opponent sideways, typically targeting the eyes. As a result, the defeated carabao always end up blind. It is also common for the winner to chase the losing carabao. They run round and round and would only stop once the losing carabao fell to the ground. Even though I enjoy watching two male carabaos fight, I did not want our own to be involved in such a bloody incident. Our male carabao was castrated when he was still young. He was strong in the field, but he was also as meek as a lamb when not at work. I loved our carabao, and I did not want him to be harmed. If he had been involved in one, he more likely than not would end up losing at least an eye. Luckily, he was able to complete his life without being involved in a fight.

It has been said many times that my father was a farmer, and we were fortunate to have owned parcels of land that we used as farms. As a part of the norm during our time, being born as a boy meant being a helping hand on the farm, and that was not a problem for any of my parents' sons. My elder brothers, Antonio and Jose, joined my father in his farm duties years before I did. As such, they were more knowledgeable about farm works than I was.

I considered it an advantage because instead of one, three people can walk me through the activities of being a vaquero.

I started herding carabaos when I was just five years old. I used to come with my elder brothers, Antonio and Jose, and watch them do the work until I finally learned to do it on my own. WWII delayed the school's opening, which gave me plenty of time to spend on the farm. When the school finally opened, I had to focus on my studies during weekdays and thus, was only able to herd our carabaos on weekends. During my younger years, I always had to come with my elder brothers, but I was so eager to do the job alone. So, after I successfully managed a herd of carabaos alone, my parents allowed me to herd the animals independentlyshortly after.

Being a vaquero was more fun than exhausting. Probably because there was nothing much that we can do during the times of WWII, but I really enjoyed most of the time that I spent on the farm. By staying with the carabaos alone, without my father and my brothers, I learned to ride the carabaos back. I was able to tame a baby carabao, which I considered a remarkable feat back then. It felt like I was in a rodeo, taming horses. Though it was fun, it definitely wasn't easy. I fell from the carabaos back many times, but fortunately, I never got hurt badly. On one occasion, I even fell with my head first. I was really lucky that I didn't get any serious injury. I consider that event as one unforgettable experience on the farm.

From Land Preparation to Harvest Season

Many people and animals were involved in farming—from the land preparation to the harvesting of rice and other major crops. Back in our time, we had no machinery to ease our farm works, so manpower was really important. Besides, farming was the primary livelihood back then so the involvement of many was not that surprising at all. In Panganiban, the available land for agriculture was still limited compared to its population. Nonetheless, every family was still able to secure farmland, even just a small parcel that was enough for their food and livelihood requirements. Other families who had bigger parcels of land were fortunate, of course. However, it also meant that they would have a bigger farmland to work on during preparation, planting, and harvesting. As expected, their family members could not do all the works on their own, and thus, they needed to hire other townspeople to help them with the tasks.

Aside from our hardworking male carabaos, most people of our community were grouped into several categories based on their roles in the fields. There were the plowmen who prepare the land for planting. The owners of the land usually took care of the planting itself, which may be done by randomly scattering the seeds over the area, by directly planting the seeds in the field, or by growing the rice plants into a small area, and then transplanting them into the field once they achieved the desired height or age. Once harvest season came, the rice harvester would do the initial work. While our carabaos threshed the harvests, we, vaqueros, would become rice gleaners. After threshing, the rice-cleaning ladies would work to remove the debris. Then, the rice would be dried, pounded, and cooked finally. For people who are unfamiliar with the typical work in the field, what I just mentioned may sound trivial. Considering the machinery that we have now and the declining interest of youth in agriculture, that is quite understandable. Nonetheless, I want to walk you through my life, including my farm life, so I will discuss the specific steps and procedures in rice farming.

The presence of our carabaos was very much appreciated from the planting season until the harvest. During land preparation, they help us plow the rice fields. Back then, we had no tractor or any machines that could help ease the activity. The only reliable option was using a wooden plow, which we call *araro.* Male carabaos would pull the *araro* forward while the vaquero follows behind to control the animal's direction. Then, back and forth, the carabao would walk until all of the fields had been plowed. It was a tedious task, but without our animals, it would have been a lot harder! Unlike the Amish people of Pennsylvania and the farmers from other underdeveloped countries back then, we did not have horses to help us in the field. More so, the farm mechanization in the U.S. was still far from our reality. Nonetheless, we still considered ourselves fortunate for having our farm best friends—our carabaos.

Preparing the field was not as easy as it seems. Thankfully, our town had the plowmen who were professional in this activity. As mentioned earlier, plowing in Panganiban was done using the *araro. Araro* was specifically designed to be used by the plowman and his carabao. It was a structured wood with steel assembly attached to it. To achieve its function of turning over the soil and making furrows, our *araro* had a sharp-pointed front with an inclined plowshare. With the carabao and the *araro* attached to it, the plowman would continue on his farm duties. The first step was to plow the fields by letting the carabao walk back and forth over the area. Once plowed, the next step was to harrow the field by using another improvised farming machine. Locally, we called it *karmot.* As far as I can remember, our *karmot* was an eight-by-eight feet structure made of wood. There was a series of teeth in one of its sides, and in its middle was an intermediate flank of wood.

Again, the *karmot* was pulled by our versatile animals, going around the field to clean it from debris. After harrowing, the land would be soft and friable yet still unready for planting. So, to make it ready, the plowman would do another round of plowing and harrowing. This was done repeatedly until the field was smooth all over. Then, the plowman would make furrows parallel to one another, from one side of the farm to another. After the plowmen's hard work, the farms would be ready to be planted with rice, corn, or sweet potatoes. For all of these crops, the same land preparation was employed.

Planting was easier than plowing, and as such, could be done by the members of the family. In general, rice planting was done through scattering, direct seeding, and transplanting. But for the other crops, direct planting provided a significant advantage because it prevents overcrowding. Like how too many people concentrated in one area leads to resource scarcity, overcrowding in plants also deprives them of their needed nutrients. Planters typically carried a container of rice and corn seeds to minimize the need to go back and forth to where they placed their tools and belongings. To ensure that the plants would be equally spaced, the planters would only drop their seeds along the furrow, with a certain distance. They did not use any measuring device for this. They just used their planting experiences to estimate the ideal space for each type of crop. After placing the seeds, they would cover the holes with soil to ensure that the seeds would not be eaten by birds. Back then, there were still birds everywhere, on the lookout for the abundance of seeds on the ground. Because the planters need to bend their backs over and over again in the course of planting, it is normal for them to feel back pain afterward. Filipinos even have a song for rice planting with the title *Magtanim Ay Di Biro,* which, in English, means that 'planting rice is not simple.' While it was true that traditional rice planting was tedious, it did not mean that the activity was boring. Planting did not take Panganibanons that long. If there were many planters available, planting would be finished in a short time. Also, while the adults were planting the crops, the younger kids in the community would stay in the field, playing guitar while singing happy and lively songs. The kids provided joy to the planters' hearts, making their work more fun and enjoyable than it was tiring. During our days as farmers and vaquero, we still did not have irrigation, so we had to rely on the merciful God for His blessing in the form of rain. The rain provided the newly-planted seeds with the water they needed, which helped the seeds germinate and grow.

I was twelve years old when I started plowing the field. I worked with my two older brothers, Antonio and Jose, while our youngest brother watched the remaining herd graze on the pasture. While we attended our farm duties, my mother and my four sisters worked on the household chores. They were busy cleaning the house, washing our clothes in the river, and preparing meals for us. Every day, the tasks seemed unending, but we never felt tired because we worked as a family, as a team, and as one.

After a few months, the harvest season for our rice plants would come. Harvesting was much easier than land preparation and planting. With our sharp semicircular knife in hand, we cut the rice plant's upper part and leave its lower part on the ground. Once all had been harvested, we would again seek the help of our carabaos for the threshing. Threshing refers to the process of separating the grains from the plant. In our case, this step separated the grains of *palay* from the rice panicle. To start with the threshing, we would let our carabaos walk over the harvest. We would lead them to walk over it back and forth until all the grains were separated from the plant. The grains were then cleaned by placing them in a large woven tray, tossing them to the air, and letting the wind blows off the dirt and the undeveloped grains. After this step, what would remain were only the good *palay*, ready for drying. We would spread the grains on a mat and let the sun do its work. After drying, the next and final step was pounding. Using mortar and pestle, the dried grains would be pounded to remove the husks. We were told that the longer you pound the grains, the whiter the resulting rice would be. It wasn't a problem for us, though, because pounding with friends and families was really an enjoyable thing to do.

Everyone in Panganiban was excited whenever the harvest season comes. Like other Southeast Asian countries, rice was our staple food, and as such, was considered the main harvest of the year. Unlike in Western countries, we do not have four seasons in a year. We do not have spring, summer, fall, and winter. We have only two—the summer season when the rain is rare, and the rainy season when the storms and typhoons often visit us. In our locality, rice was usually planted and harvested twice a year, in the months of November and December and April or May. The first harvest season of the year was a happy season for everyone, children and adults alike. It often coincided with the Easter season, the next celebration that we observed after Christmas and New Year.

As was mentioned, rice was harvested by the professional harvesters in Panganiban. They formed a group of men and women who were so good at harvesting that they could finish everything within the same day. They used an improvised knife that is similar to a scythe. In Panganiban, we called this tool an *asyab. Asyab* was so sharp that it could cut several rice panicles with one glide. Unlike corn that is picked during harvest, rice required us to cut the plant in two— the upper part containing the grains, and the lower part left on the ground. Because rice plants are small, about our knees' height, harvesting them was literally back- breaking, just the same as planting. However, since harvest also meant the return of the farmers' investments and hard work, none of the harvesters endured just another day on the farm.

The harvesters would place their harvest on a surface where they can be manually threshed by our carabaos. As our carabaos thresh the grains from the panicles, we, vaqueros, worked part-time as rice gleaners. As rice gleaners, we would go over the fields and pick the remaining rice panicles that were left and missed by the harvesters. Carrying a basket, we would search all over the field and collect as many as we could. After our baskets were filled, we would empty them in a corner and go back to the filed once again.

When there is nothing left to be picked, we would then thresh our panicles using hands. To turn the grains into cash, we would pass by the store on our way home and sell the rice grains. And so, the vaqueros found an excellent side hustle during the harvest season.

For most landowners, their harvest did not end with threshing because selling ready-to-cook rice provided better income than selling the grains. It also allowed the families to save some from their own use. And this was where the role of the rice-cleaning ladies enters. Because threshing was not just done manually but also in a not-so-clean manner, the grains required additional cleaning done by the ladies in Panganiban. To do this, they put the threshed grains in a shallow, winnowing basket. They would then throw the grains in the air and allow the wind to blow away the remaining debris and dirt from the threshing. The rice-cleaning ladies had to do it over and over until the grains became freed from debris. Sadly, the rice-cleaning ladies could not do their work whenever there was no blowing wind around.

After cleaning, drying would then proceed. Unlike our harvest, the landowners of the big parcels of land had a higher yield that required a bigger mat and a bigger surface for drying. They had to find or create that space because they could not proceed without their grains being dried. Like how the wind was crucial to the ladies, the heat of the sun was as important for the drying process. The farmers in Panganiban relied on the sun because there were no other options to have the grains dried.

Once dried, the final step was to pound the rice. As mentioned, pounding was performed by using a mortar and pestle. This step was done to remove the white grains from the husk.

Obviously, the husks would be disposed of or burned while the collected grains would be cooked for the family or sold to earn some money. For farmers who really had a huge harvest, manual pounding was not a good option. Instead, they had to go to the town, bring their already dried grains, and have them milled. Nowadays, rice mills are almost everywhere, but back in our days, there was none close to our farmlands. Fortunately, there was one small rice mill in town, and it provided its services to the farmers who needed its help. In return, the mill owner was paid a certain amount of rice for every sack of grains brought in for milling.

The Hidden Joy of Farm and Fields

Before I started high school, I had the opportunity to herd seven carabaos, two of which were males, and five were females. When not grazing or working, our carabaos were kept in a barn in our backyard. Because I was assigned to feed and look after them, I had to wake up early every day and herd my carabaos to a nearby meadow. There, they would graze the green grasses and drink the fresh water from a nearby river. Sometimes, when the carabaos had already fed on all the grass in the meadow close to our home, I would then need to bring them further away, near the foot of the mountain in Camonohan, close to our farm, and just next to Sara-Saraan.

Camonohan and Sara-Saraan were three kilometers from our home in the town proper. My father so happened to own parcels of land there where we planted highland crops like banana, cassava, corn, and malanga. Because there was no other form of transportation back then, we had to travel barefooted from town. Making our journey even more difficult were the baskets that we carried. As anyone who has climbed a mountain before will understand, the terrain going to the hill was not easy. So, to maximize the travel from the town to the farms, we always carried many baskets at once. We had one on top of our heads, two baskets placed in our shoulders, and two more that we took by our hands. These baskets must be filled with the harvests so that we would not need to go back and forth, especially considering the rugged terrain. Back then, I used to think how was it that the longer we walked, the heavier our loads became. Soon, I realized that it was probably because our muscles were already tired and thus, cannot perform as good as it did when we just departed from the farms. Despite these challenges, never can I recall a moment when my siblings and I complained about picking our harvests from Camonohan and Sara-Saraan.

Of all the good memories I had in Camonohan, there was an unforgettable one which I used to call the miracle at the stream of Camonohan. While going back to town with all the harvests from our farm, my siblings and I felt really tired of all the loads that we had on our back and shoulders. So, with the approval of all, we decided to stop by the other farm owned by my family in Camonohan. The location of that farm was very beautiful, especially with the sun shining brightly. The place was covered with different crops like banana, coconut, and sugarcane. We also had a small cottage that sat beside a stream of fresh, running water.

My siblings and I decided to rest under the shade of a tree near the stream. We were enjoying the time when, without any reason at all, the stream ran dry, right before our eyes! What surprised us even more were the freshwater rock shrimps and blackfish crawling and jumping to gasp for air. Without any word, we all jumped to where the stream was flowing just a while ago and collected all the shrimps and fish that we could. We did not stop until all of our baskets were filled. We were so happy and excited! As soon as we loaded all of our baskets, the stream went back, as quick as it ran dry a moment before. I consider the experience a once-in-a- lifetime. From that moment on, I developed this belief that miracles do sometimes happen in life.

Going from town to Camonohan was relatively less difficult, but climbing up to our farm in Sara-Saraan required more effort. I have mentioned that during the Japanese occupation, we decided to stay in our wooden house near our farm in Camonohan. But after WWII and when things finally got back to normal, we decided to return to our house in the town proper because resources were more accessible from there. And so, whenever I needed to bring my carabaos to our farms in Camonohan and Sara-Saraan, I needed to exert extra efforts. Nonetheless, the peacefulness and beauty of the place made the trek worth it.

I remember the days when we had no classes and my elder brothers and I stayed with my father on the farm to eliminate the hassles of going back and forth to the town. Whenever we went to our farm in Sara-Saraan, we always had to face a series of obstacles as what I considered them to be. Because there were still lots of plants and trees back then, we needed to follow the route of the flowing stream in order to reach our destination. The stream flows from the mountain top, and so we had to follow it in the opposite direction. Doing so wasn't easy at all. At times, I had to jump over giant boulders, so huge that they were almost four times my height as a kid. I had to move from rock to rock just so I can pass by this part of the route. The trek was really challenging, but once we reached the top, it all became worth it.

We had a nipa hut near our farm in Sara-Saraan. My father built it at the bottom of a slope, beside a flowing stream. Its location was so peaceful and quiet that I considered it similar to a magical place. The opposite side of our farm was a virgin forest, which, for me, looked like a rainforest. There were towering trees and undisturbed vegetation. The forest was a habitat for several species of birds, with varying colors and looks. It so happened that besides our hut, there was a big and tall *dapdap* tree. It was leafless, but fascinatingly, it had lots of orange-red flowers. This particular tree attracted the birds from the neighboring forest, providing us with inexplicable scenery. Their chirps were music to my ear, and their colors were rainbows to my eyes. Then the darkness started to fall. With no other light sources, I was able to enjoy the bright, twinkling lights of the night sky. The sounds of the insects and birds were like choirs. The marvelous sight and the place's peacefulness always put me to sleep, forgetting my tiredness from a day's worth of work.

I could not always take my carabaos with me, especially on the mountain top. But whenever I was around, being vaquero was my vocation. Because I was too invested in my duties as a vaquero, I actually felt sad when my carabaos could not do their usual grazing routine. This often happened when the skies were gray due to upcoming rain or typhoon and when the fields which they often grazed upon were already planted with crops such as sweet potatoes, rice, and corn. Nonetheless, herding carabaos was not a boring task because aside from me, several other boys were doing the same job as mine. They were my neighbors, classmates, and friends, so we really got along well with one another. Every time we met each other in the meadow, we would let our carabaos graze for a moment while we set our spirits free. We would climb up the hill and enjoy the relaxing breeze up there. We would enjoy watching our carabaos as they freely graze in the open pasture. We would romp and play together until we get tired and hungry. Then, we would climb up the hill once again to find any available fruits from the wild trees around. One time, we were playing in the field close to my father's coconut plantation. After playing and running around, we decided to get fresh coconuts to quench our thirst and hunger. Coincidentally, my friends Primo and Leonardo were both excellent climbers. They can climb coconut trees effortlessly, so we decided to continue our plan.

As vaqueros, we had a unique way of knowing which coconuts were ready to be picked. By simply tapping their shell, we can say from the sounds produced which were in the perfect stage for our specific needs. And so, my two friends climbed up the tree and picked the best coconuts based on their coconut-tapping skills. When all the tender coconuts were already on the ground, we opened them up one by one. Vaqueros always carry a machete when herding carabaos. The machete could be of many uses, but in our case, for that particular day, we used them to open our fresh beverage. Each of us made a small opening, just enough to drink the sweet and fresh juice inside the giant nut. Then, we cut the coconut open to get the jelly- like meat inside. After a tiring work-and-play day, we got the snack and beverage that we deserved!

Coconut is a tree that is very close to the heart of Filipinos. Aside from its juice and meat, every other part of it can also be used for various purposes. *Tuba* is one of these. *Tuba* is an alcoholic beverage made from several species of palm trees. *Tuba* gatherers collect sap from the palm trees, which they then let to ferment for at least two days. The natural yeasts present in the air ferment the sap, creating a fragrant, sweet, and mildly-intoxicating wine. If fermented for two days, the *tuba* would have at most 4% alcohol content. People who prefer a stronger beverage can further distill *tuba* and let it stand for a longer period, creating a stronger, sour, and more acidic drink that we locally call *lambanog*. If fermented further, the plain sap would be turned into vinegar.

Tuba was an original product of the Philippines, but when the Spaniards came to the country and got a taste of it, they decided to introduce *tuba* to their other colonies, including Marianas, Guam, and Mexico. Back then, the local alcoholic beverage was produced by locals in the Philippines and was then transported to their other territories through the Manila Galleons. The flavor of *tuba* found its way to the heart of foreign countries and remains popular since its initial introduction.

My brother Jose was an experienced *tuba* gatherer. He was an expert in climbing coconut trees and in collecting its sap for tuba. My father's coconut plantation gave my elder brothers ample opportunities to practice and perfect the art of *tuba* gathering.

Because our farm was situated three kilometers from town, my two brothers and I used to walk on foot to reach our plantation. During school vacations, my entire family would herd our carabaos and stay in Camonohan for the day. *Tuba* was the favorite beverage of adults, and as such, offered our family a good source of income. For us kids, we loved to have the early morning drops. I can still remember the beverage's light red color because of the added barkwhich enhanced its color and taste.

To collect *tuba* from our coconut trees, my father used to hire professional tuba gatherers. Normally, they followed a fifty-fifty sharing, which meant that if the gatherers were able to collect one hundred gallons in a day, fifty of those gallons would be ours, while the rest would be given to them as the payment. They gathered the coconut sap every morning because it was common knowledge that juice collected during early mornings was sweeter. On the contrary, the *tuba* that was collected in the afternoon was known to be sour and a bit bitter. Though gatherers might not have known the explanations behind it, their observations on the association between the time of collection and the taste are actually proven by science, chemistry to be exact!

Every afternoon, my elder brothers and I would go to Camonohan to pick up the collected *tuba.* Riding on our carabao's back, we would carry the gallons of the freshly collected coconut sap using *darikhon,* two long bamboo tubes that straddled over the back of our carabaos. Once we got home, our mother would take the collected *tuba* to the neighborhood store, and in return, my mother would be paid some amount for the supply and delivery. And for our time and effort, our mother would give each one of us two cents—for me to buy candies and for my brothers to buy their personal needs.

I, myself, was not good at *tuba* gathering. I had proven it one time when I tried to climb a coconut tree in our backyard. It was the same tree where my brother Jose practiced his coconut-climbing skills, and I expected to achieve the same. But the experience turned out more tragic than helpful. One time, I climbed the coconut tree in our backyard. Upon reaching the top, I suddenly fell off like how Humpty- Dumpty's great fall on the wall! It was another lucky moment of my life because this time, I was saved by the palms. As I fall, three palm leaves fell off with me. Thinking about it now, I realized that those palms actually saved my life! They increased the air resistance, slowed down my fall, and absorbed the shock that could have caused me serious injuries. I cannot help but be thankful for the many occasions that my life had been saved!

The Lessons—The Good and the Bad

There was one farmer whom the farmers in Panganiban, or even of the neighboring towns, admired. He was an old man known by the name Tang Engo. He did not reside in town nor was he connected to any known individual in Panganiban. Nonetheless, he was popular for his knowledge and wisdom when it comes to farming.

Like most people of his generation, Tang Engo got his wisdom not from schools but from his rich experience. Even before the Second World War, it was already challenging to send children to school because of the prevailing poverty. Most families, especially during his time, focused on survival and food. For them, learning livelihood practices such as farming was already enough. Looking at it now, I consider Tang Engo as a human chest that held not materials but intellectual treasures that were most useful for the farmers of Panganiban.

Tang Engo owned a vast property, which I estimate to be several hectares of land. His farm was about three kilometers from town, about the same distance as ours in Camonohan and Sara-Saraan. Interestingly, Tang Engo was very good at securing his farm from unwanted visitors. Surrounding his land were dense vegetations, so dense that nobody could go through to head for his farm. The only entrance that Tang Engo provided was a gate alongside a river. Whenever we want to go to him, we would need to follow this river's route just so we could find his farmland.

Tang Engo had a wife whose name was Nang Enka. Tang Engo and Nang Enka did not have a biological child, but they did have an adopted one. Because of their expansive farm, they could plant many crops within one planting season. As such, they typically grew banana, coconut, corn, peanut, rice, sugarcane, sweet potatoes, and vegetables and herbs. They also had different livestock such as poultry and swine. They lived in a barn within their farmland, and this barn became a special place for us children. Whenever the kids in Panganiban visited Tang Engo, he would gather us all in front of his humble barn and teach us about all the farming techniques that he knew about.

As a child, I learned a lot from Tang Engo. One of the most important and memorable ones was the concept of crop rotation.

Tang Engo taught us that we should not plant the same crop, on the same land, for two consecutive seasons. According to him, doing so would result in a poor harvest, pest infestation, or disease infection. I do not know if Tang Engo knew the scientific basis of such phenomena, but upon studying agriculture, I learned that they were, in fact, due to the loss of nutrients in the soil and persistence of pest and disease-causing organisms because of the presence of their hosts, which in that case, is the crop planted for two consecutive seasons.

Another important lesson that Tang Engo shared with the children of Panganiban was reusing the plant debris as natural fertilizers. As a custom, most farmers in town burn their waste to clear their fields with less effort and time. But Tang Engo was not one of them. Tang Engo used to plow his field so that the debris and remains of the harvested plants would go underneath the soil. With the help of soil organisms, those natural materials would decay and turn into natural fertilizers, making the soil rich and ready for the next planting season. Tang Engo also had a compost pit on one side of his farm. He used to collect the manure of his poultry and swine and again turn them into natural fertilizers.

The time of working in the field was also crucial for Tang Engo. To avoid the direct heat of the sun, he worked during early mornings and late afternoons. If the day was scorching, he would then just delay the work for tomorrow. Another unusual practice of Tang Engo was plowing his field at night when the moon was shining bright and the rest of Panganiban was already deeply asleep. So, by the next morning, Tang Engo would need not to plow his land any more; he would proceed directly to planting.

As a child, there is no way I could prove whether the lessons imparted to us by Tang Engo were effective or not. Of course, my father still managed and supervised our farm. Nonetheless, I was confident that his teachings were credible because he always had a good harvest throughout the entire cropping year. Even when other farmers were struggling, Tang Engo was still able to keep his harvest bountiful!

While there were good farming lessons when I was a child, there were also bad ones. As I have said earlier, Panganiban was such a beautiful place, surrounded by rich natural resources. The tall mountain served as a backdrop to our small town. On a clear day when the sun is high, these mountains looked majestic as they were kissed by the passing clouds. Big and small birds hovered over the jungle, making the place looked very much alive. The people in town loved and appreciated our mountains, but when scarcity came, they had no choice but to claim a part of the land to provide for their families' needs.

When the Japanese came, most of the people in our community decided to move from town to the mountains surrounding us. We were no more safe from our homes in town, so the only option that we had was finding a new one. Lucky for my family, we already had lands and wooden houses on our farms. However, the situations of our neighbors and relatives were different.

One day while appreciating the beauty surrounding me, I was surprised to see the mountain burning. Everywhere I looked, there was billowing smoke from more than a hundred fires. Hurriedly, I ran to my father and asked why the mountain was burning. I soon learned that the townspeople hiding in the mountain cut the vegetation there to secure land for their farming practices. When the cut trees and plants were dried, they set them on fire to totally clear their areas. Many of the townspeople resorted to this system because for them, it was an easy way of farming. As a result, I saw the mountain burning with that amount of fire and smoke for the first time in my life.

Soon enough, I learned that what the townspeople were actually doing was called *kaingin. Kaingin* is a farming system that involves cutting down trees and burning them afterward. In this farming system, farmers move from one area to another until the used land regenerate its nutrients. In other countries, *kaingin* is called swidden farming, but regardless of how it is called, it still uses the same practices and has the same consequences to the people around the area.

One thing that amazed me as a child was that when an area was being burned out, it was surprising that never did the fire extended to other parts that were not supposed to be cleared out yet. After the fire was extinguished, the farmer would clear the land of any remaining debris, and soon enough, the land would be ready for planting. They can plant any type of crops—banana, corn, cassava, coconut, elephant ears, papaya, sugarcane, and sweet potatoes. Another miraculous thing for me was that once those crops were planted, the farmers never needed to water their plants because the rain would do the work for them!

Shortly after the Japanese came to town, the once beautiful landscape around Panganiban turned into a bald mountain. At that time, the people were only concerned about their livelihood and survival that they forgot to consider the long- term effects of their actions. So one time, the reality hit us directly in our faces. As far as I can remember, a very strong typhoon hit Panganiban at that time. The typhoon brought heavy rain that poured for several days. Typhoons were not unusual in our town mainly because we were facing the Pacific Ocean. However, the impact of that specific typhoon was different. All the houses, trees, and vegetation in Panganiban were destructed. And what made the situation even worse was that, after the typhoon had passed, the town was under a flood of five- to-ten feet high. The flood was not just rainwater; it also contained mud carried from the mountain down to our beloved town. Even the giant trees that fell due to the strong wind was carried down from the mountain! The families in town were saved from a day of collecting firewood from the mountain; however, they were not saved from the river-like flood that stayed in town for some days.

That great flood, as I call it, happened so quickly that we could not process its root causes immediately. However, after a short while, it became apparent that the practice of the *kaingin* was its actual cause. Because the trees in the mountain were cut and burn, there was nothing more to absorb the water coming from the rain, and in this case, the typhoon. So the water flowed downward, with the town acting as its catch basin. There were also no more roots to hold the soil in its place. As a result of days of heavy rain, the mountain's soil became soaked and saturated until it cannot hold itself anymore. Considering the sloping terrain and the force of gravity, it was no surprise that the typhoon caused the landslide, giving our town its fair share of mud.

Thankfully, when the Japanese surrendered and left the country, the townspeople could reclaim their freedom and properties in town. Like us, they went back to town and continued their forms of livelihood back there. Not long after, the *kaingin* system slowly disappeared in Panganiban.

The Women of Panganiban

It is not trivial to many how women were deprived of their rights historically. Until they learned to fight for their rights, they were treated as inferior and were not allowed to vote nor participate in some aspects of society. In the U.S., it was only in 1920 that women earned their right to vote through the suffragist's advocacy. In some countries, women were made slaves; others used them for pleasure. Thankfully, this part of the history ended, and women are now given the right, appreciation, and recognition that they so well deserve!

Back in Panganiban, mothers and sisters were well-loved. They may not have the political and social rights that they had now, but still, they were very much valued and appreciated as part of the families. I, for one, can testify to that. Without my mother who loved me so dearly, I do not know what I would have become. My sisters also helped my mother took care of us and the household. Though they were not always with us on the farm, I knew that their chores were not easier than ours, the boys in the family.

The women of Panganiban were mostly busy taking care of the house. They cleaned the house. They cleaned the backyard. They prepared meals for each member of the family. When anyone was sick, they were the nurses, too. If needed, they could also take over the boys' tasks as long as it would not be too tedious or dangerous for them.

One of the many activities that the women in Panganiban did was being a *lavandera*. During my childhood, we had no other sources of water aside from rivers or dug-up wells. The families with a well in their backyard enjoyed the luxury of washing their clothes close to home. As for the other women, they had to carry their pile of laundry to the river on the western side of town. Typically, the women in the family did the household's laundry. However, some people who had no one to ask for assistance may opt to pay others for their laundry. Obviously, our community had no washing machine and the likes during my childhood. However, we had our own set of materials to ensure that the work was done correctly and, in a way, easier.

Back in the time, it was uncommon for the water in the dug-up well to dry. Even more rare, if not impossible, was the water of the river to stop flowing or run dry. This meant that the women, young and old alike, could do their laundry any day of the week. Nonetheless, it became a custom for the *lavanderas* to collectively work on weekends. So, during Saturdays and Sundays, the *lavanderas* would wake up early and prepare what they would need for their work for the day. They would have a *plangana,* a cylindrical basin made of aluminum materials. There, the *lavanderas* would put the dirty clothes, blankets, pants, and anything else that needed washing. They would put the *plangana* on top of their head to easily carry it to the river. They would also need to bring their bar soap and *palo-palo,* a wooden tool with a flat head and a circular handle, like an elongated table tennis racket, only that the *palo-palo* is bigger, heavier, and is made from tough wood. Some *lavanderas* would also carry a small, wooden chair so that their back won't ache for squatting by the river for a whole day. With everything ready and packed, off the *lavanderas* would go to the river.

Typical children nowadays probably do not know the traditional ways of washing clothes. That is not their fault anyway because the machines we have are supposed to ease our daily activities, including laundry. But back in my childhood days, washing clothes were still done manually. I must say that the process was unusual, but back then, that was the norm. First, the *lavanderas* would wet the dirty laundry using the flowing freshwater of the river. Then, using their bar soap, they would clean some of the laundry. They would scrub the bar soap to the clothes, rinse them a bit just enough to form the bubbles, place the dirty clothes on top of a huge stone, and, using the *palo-palo*, would pound them repeatedly. The concept behind the *palo-palo* was that by using a heavy tool and striking strong enough, repeatedly, the dirt would be squeezed out of the laundry. For the stained and white clothes, they had to undergo an extra step. Without knowing the scientific basis, it was a custom to sun-bleach the white clothes by rinsing them in the water and then laying them flat under the scorching heat of the sun. For the stained laundry, *calamondin*, a small citrus, was squeezed on the stained area to help the sun in its bleaching task! And you would not believe how effective these practices were. We needed no chlorine or any chemical; what we needed was everything that nature provided.

Though I did not experience it myself, I know for sure that being a *lavandera* was not an easy task. They needed to squat for a long time just so they could wash the clothes using the river's running water. They also needed to work under the sun's heat because, for one, the tropical sun was a helper for them. After finishing everything, they had to carry the washed clothes back to their homes and hang them dry again under the sun. Ironing was also a task for the *lavanderas.* But to make their final products perfect for wearing, they further treat the washed clothes prior to ironing. Generally, starch was used to make the clothes stiff. For the white ones, we had a blue-like liquid, which we used to call indigo. The indigo made the clothes whiter after ironing. Even thinking about the tasks of the *lavanderas* makes me tired. Considering the soil and dirt that are often in our clothes from the farm, I realized that it was like magic how our mother and sisters were able to turn them clean again as if they were not soiled in the first place!

Chapter 8

The End of the Second World War

The Second World War is considered the biggest war in history. Of all the wars that we have encountered so far, WWII claimed the most lives. To emphasize how devastating this event was, the Great War claimed 20 million lives, the Civil War caused the death of 620,000 Americans, but the Second World War? 75 million! Before it broke out, most countries were still trying to maintain and negotiate peace because they thought that the number of casualties of the Great War was already at the peak. Little did they know that it wasn't even half of the devastation that was to follow.

Germany felt that they were humiliated as a nation when they were stripped of some of their rights. As a result, they blindly put the infamous Adolf Hitler into power. They supported his leadership in expanding the German territories for the "master race." Initially, they succeed in claiming most territories in Europe, but their pursuit of Poland led to France and Great Britain declaring another war. It was in 1939 when WWII officially started, and from there, a cascade of deadly and devastating events followed.

With its war weapons and effective war techniques, Germany easily defeated France, one opponent which they thought would be hard to overthrow. After such an easy victory, Germany's confidence in themselves grew even more, especially since no more countries were standing against their expansion aside from its lone opponent—Great Britain. The events that followed make me consider Great Britain as a country that changed the course of history. Of course, I was not knowledgeable about the complexities of the war when I was a child. All I knew were the locals of Panganiban, the Japanese, and the Americans. But upon growing up, I learned about the personalities that shaped the course of WWII, the war that played a very significant part in my life. Among the world leaders that were involved, it was Winston Churchill that I genuinely admire.

When Germany was inevitably advancing their territories in the countries surrounding them, Great Britain, headed by Churchill, firmly stood against Hitler's conquest. Even when all other nations were hopeless, and it seemed that Germany had superior military power, Churchill still pursued the fight not just for Great Britain but also for other countries claimed by Germany. There were countless deaths on both parties along the way, but there was no stopping unless one of them surrender.

Probably because of the limited technologies of the time, I learned that there were several loopholes in the decision made by all the countries involved in the war. For Germany, one of its crucial mistakes was to go against its supposed "ally," the Soviet

Union, and attack one of its cities, the Stalingrad, now known as the Volgograd. Thinking that the Soviet Union was a weak nation, Germany advanced on its eastern borders until it soon learned an important lesson. Despite the Russians' military inferiority, their camaraderie and utter despise of Hitler's oppression made them won the Battle in Stalingrad. Soon enough, the Soviet Union was able to push and attack the German military backward.

By this time, the Japanese had already declared war with the U.S. after the bombing of Pearl Harbor. For this act alone, President Roosevelt earned an excuse to aid the British in their fight against Germany while at the same time fighting their own battle in the Pacific. So, after some time fighting alone, Great Britain finally earned new allies from the U.S. and Canada. Together, these three countries also attacked Germany on another side, dividing the German military power into two—one fighting the Russians and one facing the combined forces of Great Britain, U.S., and Canada.

Several battles followed, claiming millions of lives and properties from both the military forces and the civilians. But just a year after, Germany was brought to its knees after its leader, Hitler, committed suicide, and the country finally surrendered!

In the Pacific, the situation was not any better. During WWII, Japanese occupied several countries in the Pacific, including, of course, the Philippines. In all of the occupied nations, the Japanese made sure to show their power by committing crimes and atrocities. I, myself, was not unfamiliar with these wrongdoings, so it is easy for me to empathize with the other countries that the Japanese took possession of.

Since the war was initially declared against the U.S., the Americans naturally responded. They accepted the war, which they did not invite in the first place. During the first encounters, the Japanese won the battles against the U.S. because the Japanese back then were so driven by their fury. Japan was so angry about being mistreated by the Western powers and was firmly against how Japan was prevented from expanding its territories to other Asian countries. For them, if the Westerners could colonize Asian countries, why could they not? The Japanese were, literally and figuratively, dying to prove to the world that, like the nations in the West, they could also rise and be a superpower. And Japan really did! If not for its atrocities and if it only did it the right way, Japan could have been as wealthy and powerful as the U.S. and the U.K.

Sadly, the Japanese were so abusive and aggressive that there was no way that other nationalities could tolerate them. So, what the U.S. did was take hold of the territories around Japan to prevent them from further expanding. From their positions, U.S. fighters tried to enter the borders of Japan but were welcomed by a strong and fierce Japanese military. The U.S. tried for a while, but upon realizing that pursuing their entry would only delay the war, they decided to use their air power. Soon, the Americans showered Tokyo, the capital city of Japan, with firebombs. After reading historical accounts and watching documentaries, I learned that Tokyo's firebombing created a seeming inferno on land! It put the place on fire. Reports also claimed that the fire's rising smoke carried the scent of the burning flesh, turning the stomachs of the firefighter pilots. In two days, the U.S.'s city firebombing claimed at least 80,000 civilian lives!

The number would send chills to anyone, but comparing it to the murdered victims of Japanese, the number would seem insignificant. From the year 1937 to the end of WWII, it was estimated that the Japanese killed around 3 to 10 million people mostly composed of Chinese, Indonesians, Koreans, Indochinese, and Filipinos. A few months later after the Tokyo firebombing, the U.S. demanded Japan to surrender unconditionally. By the accounts of the people who were studying WWII, some claimed that the Japanese were ready to surrender conditionally. In contrast, others argue that there were no signs of them surrendering. So, the U.S. made use of a newly developed weapon that had never been used in the history of war—the atomic bomb!

The use of the atomic bomb was also questioned by many, especially since it brought long-term impacts to the Japanese even after WWII. However, the U.S. felt the necessity to use the weapon to make Japan finally surrender. During that time, Germany was already defeated, but Japan was still pursuing the battle. So, on August 6, 1945, a U.S. bomber plane dropped the first atomic bomb in the city of Hiroshima. The event instantly killed another 80,000 civilians. Three days later, on the 9th of August, another nuclear bomb was dropped in Nagasaki, claiming40,000 lives. The Hiroshima and Nagasaki bombing marked the end of the Second World War when, on August 15, Japan's emperor announced its unconditional surrender.

Closer to home, the insurgency against the Japanese was also intense. Underground groups lived in the mountains, fighting their own battles against the Japanese. The guerilla activities were very active that, even before the end of WWII, only twelve provinces in the country were left in the Japanese's hands. Even in our small town of Panganiban, we had our own story of bravery despite the lack of military weapons and equipment. It was not surprising, though. The earlier generations of Filipino heroes were also able to defy the odds and fight against the Spaniards and Americans. We have Jose Rizal who bravely fought using his *pluma,* and Andres Bonifacio who fought blood by blood using his *bolo* and revolver.

When the Japanese heard of the Hiroshima and Nagasaki bombing, it quickly dawned on them that they were losing. Adding to their worries was the long- awaited return of Gen. Douglas McArthur to the country. When the guerillas in the mountain learned about these events, they courageously went out of their hiding places, went down to the neighboring town, and faced the Japanese soldier there. The battle happened in the Banquerohan Bridge, just one kilometer away from Panganiban. It was a hand-to-hand fight between the two groups, and by the Grace of God, the last group standing was the Filipino guerillas! By the end of the face- off, all the Japanese soldiers were in the murky water of the river; not even one survived.

For me, the fight in the Banquerohan Bridge was terrifying. But for my elder brothers, Antonio and Jose, and the kids of their age, it was worth watching. So, what they did was climb up the tall coconut trees by the hill and watch the fierce battle between the Japanese and the Filipinos. The bloody battle was something that any kid should not see, and without doubt, the historical encounter in the Banquerohan Bridge was forever remembered by the kids who got to see it.

Before the Banquerohan Bridge fight, the garrison in town where we used to buy lemon drops was set to fire by the Japanese themselves. They burned down the fort and every public building in town, probably to remove any trace of their wrongdoings. The fire consumed the entirety of the building, but miraculously enough, no other town structure was involved. As far as I can remember, it was a windy day, so it was hazardous, especially for the wooden houses and nipa huts in town. The people in town claimed seeing Saint James the Greater, our Patron Saint, was seen hovering around the burning building. The townspeople believed that once again, we were saved from what could have been another devastating event.

At Camp 18, where the coal mine was located, another bloody fight took place. The guerillas attacked the Japanese soldiers there and once again won the battle. Following the Japanese soldiers' death in Panganiban and the neighboring town, most of their bodies were seen floating in the rivers, ready to be carried away to the sea. During this period, the locals opted not to fish in the meantime, for the river was filled with blood and human carcasses! Many people became sick after the war, with scabies, a skin disease, being the most common condition. The children in town were mostly affected, and even I was not an exemption. Even until now, I could still remember how itchy and painful my scabies was!

But the disease following the war was nothing compared to the freedom that we finally regained. After defeating all the Japanese soldiers in town, Panganiban was once again free! We were free to return to our normal lives. We were free to reclaim our properties in town. We were free to start our livelihood in town. Panganiban, my beloved hometown, earned its freedom, but it did not mean that our economic conditions would be better in an instant.

One time in 1942, while children played around in the front yard of our houses, our attentions were suddenly caught by the loud sounds of the Japanese airplanes hovering on top of us. It was a cloudless day, and so the structures of the planes were so clear to use. With the loud noise taking over our peaceful neighborhood, everyone, adults and kids, went out to see what was happening around. Then, paper-like things started falling from the sky. To us on the ground, it was like a confetti of something that we were not sure of. Once they touched the ground, we quickly recognized them as money. We were showered with Japanese money! Out of excitement and surprise, everyone started picking up as many bills as they could. I gave all the money that I picked to my Nanay and Tatay, and they kept them in the box.

By the end of the war, these paper bills became invaluable and useless. There was no way my parents could ask for a replacement with actual money that could be spent in the market. For us children, it meant that we could again use the cent that we so much preferred over the bills. But for our parents, it meant working hard to earn pesos or dollars that they could spend to support the family.

After the war, food and money became even more scarce! The town's rice supply was not sufficient for its population, and so most of us had to totally or partly rely on each family's own produce. We relied on our sweet potatoes and corn in the backyard or the field. But this seemingly worst situation was even worsened by the passing of strong typhoons. Every time Panganiban was hit, most of the town's vegetation and crops were brought to the ground.

Even our houses were sometimes devastated. Whenever a typhoon passed by us, it was like starting from scratch over and over again.

Back in the time, there were no Red Cross nor Salvation Army to save the day. Everyone in the country was struggling to survive after the war. Also, since we were on an island, it was nearly impossible to expect help from the country's main islands. The only option we had was to be resilient and to stand on our own feet. Thankfully, the people in my town were as helpful as anyone could be. We value camaraderie and unity more than anything. After the war, the typhoons, and the floods, we always relied on one another and believed that the good God would take care of His creation. And thankfully, we were never proven wrong!

CHAPTER 9

FRANK'S EARLY EDUCATION

During my childhood, the Philippines' education system was still different from what was used by most countries. We had no kindergarten. We only had six years of primary education and four years for secondary. We had no junior and senior high schools yet. After these ten years, the students could directly proceed to their college education. Students typically start their education by six to seven years old, but our education was delayed because of the war.

My early education wasn't that early anymore because of WWII. Until the war was over, the schools in the country were kept close. It was what the time required. I was already eight when the war ended, and only then was I able to attend classes. As a child, I was observant and curious so, even though the schools were initially closed, I made sure that I learned practical things in life in the meantime.

As has been mentioned, the war brought extreme poverty to the locals of Panganiban. Nonetheless, it was not enough of a reason to discourage us from attending the school. Because we lack money and other materials, we relied on our resourcefulness to provide for our educational needs.

One thing that I won't forget when I started my first grade was my wearing of an improvised school uniform. Back then, there was no cotton or any other clothes available in Panganiban, and so my parents and siblings thought of a way to provide me with one. We had an abaca plantation in our farms, and knowing that abaca could be used in making fabrics, my father designed a wooden weaving machine for this purpose. The first step in making abaca fabrics was to collect the raw materials. So, my father would climb up the mountain and cut and topple down the abaca trees that were ready for harvest. Then, he would remove the stem's outer parts until he reached the whiter sheaths inside of it. Without the machine, my father used to strip these sheaths one by one using a specially designed sharp- pointed knife, which he made from the femoral bone of a carabao. He made this step easier and quicker through his wooden weaving machine.

The wooden weaving machine had steel teeth embedded in its main wooden body. These teeth were responsible for stripping the sheaths from abaca to get the fibers. It had a foot pedal that controlled the opening and closing of the teeth, which was necessary for the feeding of abaca sheaths. Then, passing through the steel teeth, one must pull the sheath with all his might and force. The resulting product of this machine were abaca fibers to be dried under the heat of the mountain sun.

Once dried, my father would bring the fibers down to town, wherein my mother and my elder sisters would continue the process. Using their skills and a sharp eye, they would tie one end of a fiber to the end of another, creating a long thread similar to a cotton thread in a spool. What amazed me was that even though the abaca fibers were tied, finding the knots along the yarn was really difficult. The knot seemed to just disappear!

Then, my father would again assemble the machine, this time, for its primary purpose of weaving the abaca fibers. Putting the unique parts for weaving was a challenging task, but nonetheless, it was worth it considering the lack of other alternatives. Before the wooden weaving machine could be put into use, the abaca fibers had to be wound on a wooden bobbin first, a feature that was not that different from the regular sewing machine. At both ends of the machine, a set of hooks must be threaded like a threading needle. For my father's wooden weaving machine, the resulting fabric was set to one yard. Weaving through the machine was hard, but my sister Luz was very good at it. In a day of work, she could weave several yards of fabric, enough to make clothes for the whole family!

So, my sister prepared the fabric for my school uniform. With my mother and sisters working together, they cut the abaca fabric just enough to fit my size. Then, using a big needle, they sew the improvised uniform by hand. By then, the abaca fabric was still stiff to be worn as a cloth so, what they did was to soak my uniform in a lime solution. After this chemical treatment, they carried my uniform to the river and pounded it repeatedly using the *palo-palo* until it became soft enough to be worn. Like regular clothes, it was then rinsed by the river's flowing freshwater and dried under the sun's heat.

And so, when the first day of school came in October 1945, all I had as a uniform was the one made from abaca fiber. It is really difficult to describe how the abaca cloth looked like. But to at least give you an idea, my uniform that day was sewn like a T-shirt, with a slit in front and hanging up to my knees. I also had school shorts made from the abaca fiber; however, it seemed that my mother did not know my size because the resulting one was too tight for me. Still, I wore the abaca shorts even though there was no more allowance for any movement. I felt like I was a paper doll back then!

Honestly, if there was any other option, I wouldn't have chosen to wear my abaca uniforms. I was shy to attend the class wearing it, but that was the only choice. My desire to learn was stronger, and so I went on to our improvised classroom. Before the Japanese left, they burned all public buildings, including the school in town. So, what served as our classrooms were residential houses in Panganiban. Upon reaching the premises, I was relieved to see that some children were also wearing abaca uniforms. I was not alone! For the rest of the children, they had another improvised uniform made from empty flour bags. Their parents worked to remove the print and formed the used bags into their children's uniforms. Had I known of this option and had my family had empty flour bags, I would have chosen to use them as uniform instead of the abaca fiber. Because of poverty and the war, our class was composed of children aged seven to twelve. I was not discouraged, though. In fact, it made me see how dedicated and invested we were in education because we still prioritized our learnings despite the poverty and the effects of the war.

Aside from the classrooms and the uniforms, there were many more improvised school materials used in our class. Our teachers had no chalk, so they used the limestones that remained from the old municipal building after it was consumed by the fire. We had no paper, so we used banana leaves instead. For the ink, the best alternative was the purple juice of a particular vine that was common in Panganiban during that time. Our glue was cooked rice or the sticky sap produced by fruit trees. Our books were not enough for the number of children, so we had to share them with our classmates. As far as I could remember, one book was shared by five to six children. Back then, there was no alternative mode of transportation yet, aside from our feet, of course. Sadly, it was extremely rare for a child to have shoes for schooling. I was one of those who had not, and so I walked barefooted together with most of the students. Thinking about it, it really amazes me how resourceful dedicated people can be! Reminiscing my early school days when almost everything was not available makes me thankful for what I have now. It makes me wonder how God watched us, the school children of Panganiban, from above, and how He provided us with nature that was enough to support our needs.

CHAPTER 10

THE UNFORGOTTEN MEMORIES OF MY YOUTH

Needless to say, WWII was unhelpful and beneficial, but despite the chaos that it had brought upon Panganiban, I and all other Panganibanons still found happiness in the simplicity of life. In this chapter, I like to walk you through the unforgotten memories of my youth, during and after the Second World War.

My first adventure was the elaboration of my earlier story about me falling from the coconut tree. The story actually goes this way. My older brother, Jose, was an excellent coconut climber. He could get from the ground to the top of the tree in no time. Putting his skills to work, my brother regularly climbed the coconut tree in our backyard every afternoon after school. I would often see him doing this routine, wondering what he had been doing there all those times. So for several afternoons, I decided to watch him closely and see what was up there that my brother was so faithful to visit. Soon enough, I found that he would prepare several things that he needed to take with him to the top before he climbed the tree.

First, he would make sure that he has his *tigpas,* a scythe with a scabbard. He would secure it around his waist, the same way the vaqueros carried theirs whenever they were out in the fields. He would also take a cylindrical tube made from a large bamboo cane, which we called *be-as.* The upper nod of the *be-as* was removed to have an opening on the top while keeping the lower nod intact. Doing this transformed the cylindrical tube into a container. My brother also attached a strap to this container so that he could carry it with his shoulder while his hands were busy climbing. Together with the *tigpas* and container, Jose also brought with him twines. Once everything was ready, my brother Jose would start his journey up to the top of our twenty-five-foot-tall coconut tree!

My brother was very skilled at this that within one minute, he would already be on top. As a child, I was always wondering how it felt to be there. Even though I had not experienced it yet, I knew for a fact that being there would give me a good view of the village and the town. This thought had always been in my mind, pushing me to do the most daring thing that I did in my whole life! But because Jose was so used to being up there, it did not give him the excitement anymore. I was sure that he was not climbing the tree to take a glimpse of the town, and so I continued my observation.

When Jose was already positioned securely on top of the palm tree, his next move was to pull the twine in his pocket, take the coconut flower, position it at a downward angle, and tie its end to the closest palm. If you have not seen one, the flowers of a coconut tree have an unusual appearance and a rather complicated structure. The flowers are enclosed in a long tubular structure, about two to three feet long, and with a sharp-pointed tip. So, once the flower structure was tied and positioned correctly, Jose would use his *tigpas* to cut the flower about two inches from its tip. After this step, the sap of the flower would start flowing down. To collect the sap, Jose would then tie the container to the other end of the flower, allowing it to hang in the air while the juice flowed down freely to his container. Upon seeing everything, I soon realized that what my brother was doing was collecting and drinking the freshly collected coconut sap, the same sap that was being fermented to make *tuba.* As mentioned before, early morning sap tastes better than the afternoon sap, but nonetheless, both make a good beverage!

After I learned what Jose was doing up there, I became even more interested in risking at least a limb to see the village from up high and to taste fresh coconut sap that I myself collected. I cannot say for sure if it was fortunate or not, but the next afternoon, my brother did not come for his afternoon routine. I had no idea why he was absent. But my curiosity pushed me to try climbing the tree myself. Coincidentally, no one was around by that time, and I was free to climb the tall coconut tree in our backyard. I did not tell my siblings nor my mother because, for sure, they would not allow me. So, I climbed the tree secretly!

After ensuring that no one was around, I started my way to the top. But upon moving closer to the tree, I realized that the trunk of the tree was too large for my small arms to hold on to. I knew it would make climbing harder, but I was determined that I decided just to proceed little by little. And so I continued as plan. I climbed the tree slowly but surely. And it was not without a reward.

Soon enough, I reached the top, and I had finally fulfilled one of my dreams! I was on the top of the world, looking down on creations, as the lyrics of Karen Carpenter's song say. It was my first time to be in a position so high that I can literally see everything around. It was my first time seeing the ground from atop of our twenty-five-foot- tall coconut tree. As I sat up there, I realized an important life lesson. The higher you go up, the better your view would be. In real life, it could also be translated as the higher your achievements, the better your life would become.

I was so consumed with the beauty that surrounded me that I did not realize that the palms I was sitting on and was holding on to were not that reliable anymore. Before I knew it, I was already on the ground, together with the three palms. There was a big boom when I hit the ground, which my Aunt Eugenia heard of. So, she came to see what happened and saw me in an unideal state. According to her, my tongue retracted that I could not cry nor speak upon impact. My aunt called my mother and my siblings, and my Nanay hurriedly fetched a pail of water and splashed it all over me. Shortly after, I started to cry.

The event caused a commotion in the backyard. Most of the neighbors came to see what happened and to check if I was alright. Thankfully, despite the height of the tree, I still ended up alive and well. My Uncle Florentino also came to our house to ensure that my body was free from injuries or fractures. To check, he lifted up my head and pressed his palms on both sides of my head. According to him, if I scream in pain, then there were dislocated bones. Thankfully, I did not feel any pain, and I did not scream, of course. Finally, we were guaranteed that all of me was still intact!

Climbing up the twenty-five-foot-tall coconut was a once in a lifetime experience. It was both unforgettable for showing me such a beautiful sight and painful for the fall that shortly followed. On that day, I was thankful for all the people that were there to help. To the neighbors who were so concerned about my life. To my aunt and uncle, who ensured that I was well and safe. To my mother and siblings, who urgently responded. And to God, of course.

On that day, I thought that these people were the only ones to be thankful for. But upon studying physics in college, I realized that the three palm trees played a crucial part in my being alive until today. I learned that the air resistance acting against the palms created a buoyant effect that reduced my impact to the ground. Together with my angels, the three palms saved me from a guaranteed death from the fall! On that day, I proved that I was not Peter Pan after all; I was more of a Humpty- Dumpty instead.

My second memory is about the fun following the devastations of the typhoon that passed by our town. As has been said many times, Panganiban was frequently visited by typhoons because the town's eastern side is facing the Pacific Ocean. By typhoons, I do not mean the typical ones. The typhoons in Panganiban were really strong and devastating. Looking in the eyes of a child like me during those times, I can say that it was like wrath from the heavens or from Poseidon from the sea. It puts all the trees down to the ground, mud from the mountains down to our town, and a river-like flood that Panganibanons were so used to seeing and experiencing.

The heavy rain of the typhoon was also accompanied by such heavy wind. When indoors, we would hear the wind's whistling sounds, so loud that it seemed like someone was whistling all around our house. Our wooden houses and nipa huts were not exempted too. If we did not secure our roofs earlier before the typhoon came, our households would likely be soaked by the heavy rain. Going outside our homes was not an option either. If one dared come out, that person must be ready to fly with the wind to a destination only the wind would know. When I was a child, my mother always reminded me not to go out of the house whenever there was a typhoon. She used to tell me the story when my elder sister was blown away by the strong wind, only to be left in our backyard, on top of the bushy and thorny bamboo trees! Until now, I cannot say for sure if the story was real or a hoax created to scare the children in the family. If it the latter, I must say that it was effective because, as a child, this story was scary enough to keep me indoors.

Aside from the rain and the wind, the sky was also part of the orchestration. Whenever a typhoon passed by our town, the whole place would be covered with thick dark clouds. For me as a child, it was like experiencing night time even in the middle of the day. We had no electricity, so it was really dark. The clouds would be covering the sun, moon, and stars, depriving us of our natural sources of light. The only light that remained were the sparks of lightning in the sky. Later on, I learned that bolts of lightning are formed due to the rubbing and collision of the particles in the clouds, creating an electric current, which we see on land as bolts of light. Though there was a low likelihood of being struck by lightning, its light, in contrast with the dark sky, was like a nightmare in the eye of a child. What made lightning even scarier for me was the thunder that shortly followed. The thunder took over the wind's whistling sounds, which did not make the experience any better.

Typhoons in Panganiban were terrifying and devastating, but we still found things to enjoy and appreciate afterward due to our resiliency. Because the town was usually flooded like a river, the townspeople thought it was a good idea to actually treat it like one! So, my father used to collect the fallen banana stem, place them side by side, and pierce them together with a bamboo cane to build a big banana raft. And what followed was one of the best experiences for us children—banana rafting in flood!

Excitedly, all the children in the neighborhood would gather in front of our house to line up for the unusual ride. Everyone was excited. My brothers Antonio and Jose were usually the captains of our raft. They would use bamboo canes to direct the bamboo raft from one end of the town to another. It was such a thrilling experience, sailing and overcoming the obstacles all over Panganiban. Along the way, some children would jump over the raft to share the ride. However, our raft could only accommodate so much. With all the children of Panganiban riding all at once, we surely would sink to the ground! So, what we usually did was to offer several trips from one end to another end of town. The children who were watching in amusement initially were also given a chance to enjoy the rafting experience that they would surely remember throughout their lives. Once we reached the trip's point of origin, which was the submerged front yard of our house, the initial passengers would get off, and a new set would embark. Of course, I had the privilege to join all the rides. Thanks to my father who made our banana raft!

The lack of technology and toys during my childhood was not an issue back then because nature provided us more than what we needed. Though I think this is not anymore the case today, but back then, kites were really popular with children. With Panganiban's vast fields, it was the perfect game for us children. However, since we were so poor during those times, we did not have the money to buy a kite. Fortunately, we learned how to make our kites using materials that were readily available in the community. So, almost all of us children used homemade kites instead.

If you have seen kites before, you should know that kites can have different forms, colors, shapes, and sizes. You can shape it as a bird, as a plane, as a dragon, or a butterfly. You can opt to use plain shapes and make them rectangular, hexagonal, or the most common diamond-shaped kites. As long as your chosen design or shape would provide the kite with enough lift and stability, then you are good to go. Kites also come in different colors. It can be made from one color only, or use as many colors as you want. Back in our time, the color of our kites depended on the availability of materials. Some kites also have tails, while others do not. In the end, it depends on what the child and the maker prefer, but in Panganiban, our kites had no tails.

To make our own kites, we only needed four materials. First, we needed bamboo strips made from parts of a bamboo cane. Since we had bamboos in the backyard, securing bamboo strips was not a problem for me. The remaining three materials were Japanese crepe paper, glue, and tiny strings. If we had none of these, we would improvise for substitute. We could also ask other kids to share their materials with us.

After ensuring that our materials were complete, the next step was to decide what specific size we would want for our kite. We would then prepare six bamboo strips—one larger strip to hold all the other parts in the middle, two long and one medium strip to hold the crepe paper, and two short pieces for the streamer. For the specific kite that we used to make in Panganiban, the actual process went like this. First, we would make the tips of the long and medium strips thin enough to be bent and tied together. As far as I can remember, we made at least six inches at the ends of the bamboo strips thin to make room for this bending and tying. Then, using the string, we would tie the tips of the two long strips to the large, central piece. The next step was to place the medium strip to the lower end of the central piece. Once tied securely, we would then connect the three strips together, creating a somewhat mixture of a semi-circular and a semi-triangular shape. Finally, the two short pieces were added to the central top part to hold the streamer. After finishing these steps, we would already have the frame of our kite. I can still remember our excitement once we reached this stage.

Because we already had the frame, we could proceed to complete the body of our kite. To do that, we would use our colorful Japanese crepe papers. The crepe papers must be securely attached to ensure that the kite would not be damaged while flying up high. We would then put the streamers on and attach the string that we would be holding on to later. The strings must be tied to the mid-upper part and the mid-lower portion of the central piece to allow the kite to tilt a little bit while flying. Even as a child, I knew that if I did not allow my kite to tilt, it would not fly high in the sky. Of course, I wanted to see my kite flying majestically above, so

I always tied my strings properly. Finally, the last step was to tie the strings in the central piece to the long string that was in our spools.

To finally set our kites in the sky, we needed a helping hand from one of our siblings or friends. One person must hold on to the spool of string while the other kid goes to a distance and give the kite a lift. He must wait for the perfect wind to blow because if the wind is too strong, it might take the kite away, and if the wind is too weak, it would just take your kite back to the ground. Once lifted, the streamers of our kite would create beautiful sounds that could attract the townspeople's attention, and together, we would watch our kite fly beautifully in the sky.

Because of our fondness for kites, we have this unusual kite-flying competition every summer. The harvest season usually came before summer, and so we could freely enjoy the vastness of the field and the blowing winds above it. So before the big day, we, vaqueros, would plan for the event. Each team would be made of two people but could only have one kite entry. Everyone was free to join, vaqueros or not. It was one of the sought-after events in summer.

The guideline for the competition goes like this. To start the event, two teams would be chosen for the first face-off. For each team, one of the members would hold the spool while the other would run to a distance to help the kite lift-off. Once on-air, the member holding the spool would control their kite to attack the opponent. By pulling the string strong enough, one can control the kite to move up and down. It was like playing the Nintendo, with the strings acting as the joystick. The kites would attack each other until one makes a hole out of the other. A kite with a hole cannot fly anymore, and so it would instantly drift back to the ground. The fallen kite was the loser, and the one remaining in the sky was announced the winner. Then, a new challenger would face the defending champion until only one kite remained. The last kite standing would be named the season's champion and would be defending the title once again in the next summer.

The kite-flying competition was such a good memory. I can still remember how many kites were there during each season. They came in different shapes and colors. Some had big, and others had even bigger. But one thing they had in common—they had no tails!

My next memory is related to the main crop of Panganiban—*palay.* In the Philippines, we have our own version of cereals, which we call *pinipig.* Before the harvest season came, my parents would collect immature green rice in the field. These were the ones that did not mature soon enough to be harvested together with most rice plants in the same area. So, instead of being wasted, my parents would collect them, and we would turn them into *pinipig.* After collection, the immature rice grains would be threshed manually and then roasted in our wooden stove at home. Once sufficiently roasted, my mother would take them out of the stove and transfer them to a huge mortar in front of our house. There, it would be pounded until they were flattened into a cereal-like texture and appearance.

Back in the days, *pinipig*-making was more of a custom than food processing. It was celebrated by young boys and girls in town who were in high school and were starting to bloom as men and women. During our time, this was also the time when a young man courts a young lady. Unlike today, courtship during those times was still done earlier because people were married younger too. Courtship was also more traditional, which followed several stages from courtship to marriage, and as I see it, *pinipig*-making used to play a crucial role in the flourishing of relationships in Panganiban.

Our house provided a perfect place for *pinipig*-making in our village. Our house had an overhang that provided shade for our big mortar, and there, the kids and youth of our village gathered. In front of our house was a *sari-sari* store. In the Philippines, every community has its own convenience store called the *sari-sari* store. These stores are often built as an extension of their owner's house and offer retail products. *Sari-sari* store has always been helpful, especially to poor families who cannot go to supermarkets and grocery stores. The same was also true for us in Panganiban. In front of our house was a *sari-sari* store, so younger kids and students always hanged out in our front yard.

On the day when the immature rice was collected, the children and youth of Panganiban would gather in front of our house. They would come in pairs composed of a girl and a boy. Those who came without a partner may choose from others who were still available. The pairs would line up and wait for their turns to make the *pinipig.* The rest who ended up without a pair would just play guitar and play love songs in the background.

After my mother roasted and placed the immature rice in the mortar, the first pair would come and pick a pestle for each of them. Then, in rhythm, they would pound the immature rice until it turned into the cereal-like *pinipig.* The pair had to be synchronized; else, their pestle would bump into each other. Later on in life, I realized that maybe it was adults' way to teach the youth of the importance of being synchronized as husbands and wives. If that is the case, then I must say that it was a wonderful way of teaching the younger generations of such an important life lesson.

Pinipig-making was a special day that the kids and youth of Panganiban enjoyed. It may just be merely pounding rice, but for us, it was a happy moment of playing guitar, singing love songs, and pounding immature rice with the girl of our dream! *Pinipig,* the final product, was eaten as cereals or used as toppings of Filipino desserts such as ice cream and *halo-halo.*

Finally, my last unforgettable experience happened while I was working as a vaquero. On that day, I just got home from school when my friend and co-vaquero, Leonardo, passed by our house. He asked me if I wanted to take our carabaos to the meadow and feed them with grass that afternoon. I looked at the sky and saw that it was clear and blue. There were white clouds that make the sky look even more beautiful. There were no signs of rain or anything that could ruin the day. So, I thought to myself, it was a perfect time to give our carabaos a treat!

And so I agreed to come with Leonardo. We took our carabaos to the field and let them graze upon the fresh green grasses all around. While our herds were busy, Leonardo and I thought of going to the nearby river to collect rock shrimps for our dinner. So on we went. On the river's sides were coconut trees, providing us the shade from the still shining sun. The birds around us were chirping loudly, creating sounds similar to a choir. Blackbirds watched us, probably expecting us to give them some fish or maybe thinking of ways to steal our catch.

We started in the shallow part of the river. However, since there were not many shrimps in there during that day, we decided to move to the deeper parts of the river. We were determined to caught rock shrimps because we already imagined it to be our viand for the night. On the other side of the bank, the rocks werebigger, and the water almost reached our knees. Since we were moving upstream against the current, we had to hold on to rocks to move forward. I was doing that very thing when, upon touching one rock, I touched something different whose form and texture were not that of a rock shrimp. In the very moment that I grabbed the unknown being, I felt a sharp, burning sensation in the tip of my hand. Instinctively, I shouted so loud that the birds sent the birds away. Leonardo instantly came to the rescue and tried to comfort me. However, the pain was too unbearable and excruciating that Leonardo's presence did not make me feel any better. While comforting me, Leonardo explained that I just touched *ngayangay,* a very poisonous fish! This fish was so defensive that once you touched its fins, it would immediately inject its poison into you. And that was exactly what happened to me on that supposedly perfect day.

Back in that day, both Leonardo and I still had no idea about first aid and the likes. Nonetheless, our instincts told us that the only thing we could do to stop the pain was to tie the rubber band that Leonardo had on his wrist. Leonardo took off the rubber band, stretched it, and wrapped it around my finger as a tourniquet. The pain did not stop immediately, but it did help prevent the poison from traveling to other parts of my body. The rubber was very helpful, but we did not know that it was not supposed to be tied for a long time. I spent the night with it and only removed the rubber the following day.

I was saved from the poison, but not from the lack of blood circulation! When I removed the rubber the following day, my forefinger was all swollen and blue due to the lack of blood for such a long period. When my sister Luz saw my condition, she immediately took me to one of our uncles. This uncle just finished his pre-med in Manila and was running a small pharmacy in town. Using his little knowledge of medicine, he gave me a penicillin shot, which helped eliminate the pain. He explained that the prolonged lack of blood circulation damaged the tissue underneath my skin for my still swollen finger.

Our next stop was to my other uncle, also named Francisco. He recommended that I undergo surgery to remove the damaged tissue. So, using his basic surgical instruments, he performed the surgery, and my finger was saved! Sadly, the poisonous fish still left me with a scarred finger and a crooked nail. Every time I look at my hands, I am always reminded of that perfect day in the fields, the poisonous fish, and my carefree days in Panganiban!

CHAPTER 11

MY HIGH SCHOOL LIFE

I cannot tell you the story of my high school life without talking about how I almost did not finish elementary. When I was in the sixth grade, and it was only a day away from our graduation, I could not clear myself from my school's responsibilities because a book that was borrowed under my name was missing! In most public schools in the Philippines, books are owned by the government and were only lent to students. At every end of the school year, students should return the borrowed books and complete all other requirements to be allowed to move to the next grade. Back then, children were only required to finish their primary education. Moving to secondary was a choice, mainly because high school was not free anymore.

As mentioned earlier, five to six students shared one book during our time. Unfortunately, the missing book was borrowed under my name, and so I carried the responsibility. The lost book was a Filipino translation of *Noli Me Tangere* or *Touch Me Not* in English. It was a book written by our national hero, Dr. Jose P. Rizal, during his fight against the Spaniards. It was initially written in Spanish but was later on translated to Filipino so that the school children could understand.

As a child, I was fond of studying, and I was so decided to attend secondary school. However, the missing book seemed to think otherwise. No matter how hard I searched, the book was still nowhere to be found. If I could not find it the day, I would need to pay for it in order to qualify for graduation. But even that option seemed impossible. My family was poor, and we had no money to pay for it. Even the thought of telling my parents about the book already haunted me that day. I was already losing hope, and the only option I had was to tell my teacher about my situation.

And so I went to Mrs. Santos, my kind and pretty teacher, and told her about my distressing situation. As nice as she always was, she made an announcement in class that whoever had or knew where the book was must return it to me that morning. When the lunch break came, I was patiently waiting for anyone to return the book to me. The clock was ticking, and every tick made me feel a little more hopeless. The lunch break ended, and still, no book came out. So, Mrs. Santos made another announcement that if the missing book was not found, then no one in the class would be included in the graduation. She said that she was expecting honesty from all of us. Everyone went silent! Before we were sent home that day, Mrs. Santos asked us to close our eyes and demanded whoever had the book to return it while no one was looking. And alas! The missing book was found! Thanks to Mrs. Santos, the whole class, including me, graduated in the year 1952!

When I started high school, I was already at the age of seventeen. It was partly because my primary education was also delayed by WWII and because of the prevailing poverty during that time. Since my family was poor and my parents needed helping hands working on the farm, my siblings and I could not simply continue our education without considering our livelihood. We had to take turns in helping our parents with fieldwork and household chores. After finishing elementary, I helped my father for two more years before I finally enrolled in high school.

I attended CAIC, a high school in Panganiban whose main curriculum was Agriculture and Fishery. That meant that our classes were not just the typical subjects like in elementary. Instead, we also had theoretical and practical classes related to crop production and aquaculture. Every morning, all the students, boys and girls, had to do fieldwork under our respective instructors' guidance. Our school had its own field, farming equipment, and even carabaos. The class needed to grow a crop of our choice, and so obviously, the boys were assigned to preparing the fields. We had to use the carabaos, *araro,* and *karmot.* Every student was required to learn how to use the equipment, which meant that everyone must do the tasks. The good thing was that even I was from a family of a farmer, and I already learned what was taught to us and had been helping in land preparation since I was twelve. In high school, I was definitely able to use the lessons taught to me by my elder brothers and my father, of course!

Since our curriculum was focused on both agriculture and fishery, we also had fieldwork on the fishery. Within the compound of or school was Panaguican, an area where the swamplands were. There were also nipa palms, mangroves, and marshes in Panaguican. There was the Panaguican Hill, a view that provided a good backdrop to the swamp if we looked farther.

Some days, we would do our fieldwork in Panaguican. From morning to noon, we had to clear the swamp from the existing vegetation. Then, we would form a pond by building dikes. Building a dike was not easy, though. We had to move the mud to the dike following the design that was initially laid out by the class. We did that by using *banka* or a wooden boat or by manually pushing and placing the mud to build the dike. Compared to land preparation, building the pond was harder for me because our muscles were still small and weak while the mud and debris were so heavy. We also did this work under the scorching heat of the sun. Nonetheless, we had no choice but to continue the work.

So, once the dike was built, the next task was to install the gates to make compartments and to control the flow of the water from each. We would open this gate during high tide to let water in. Once a certain point was reached, we would close the gate and plant the fish fries and *bangus* or milkfish. They would stay in this compartment until they grew into fingerlings. Once this stage was achieved, we would transfer the fingerlings to another compartment to allow them to grow. They were fed commercial fish meal, but they also had an abundance of algae growing from the pond.

After the morning fieldwork, we would have a break for lunch and for rest. Then, for the afternoon session, we would return to our classroom to discuss the typical subjects such as English, Math, Science, and so on. Of course, we could not just focus on agriculture and fishery; we also had to learn the basic curriculum subjects. Earning our diploma in high school was really difficult for us. In fact, during our first year, we had classmates from neighboring towns. But soon enough, only Panganibanons and those from the nearby barrios remained.

Without a doubt, the curriculum in CAIC was challenging, but we had no other choice because that was the only high school available in town. We cannot transfer to schools in other towns or in Manila because of financial limitations. In CAIC, the tuition was small, but a family without a stable income would still struggle. So, finishing our studies in CAIC was the best and the most practical option for us students and for our families.

Aside from the fieldwork, there was another subject that I was struggling with— Mathematics. As someone who graduated with honors in elementary, you may think it was odd that I was not good in Math, but that was really the case back then. In elementary, I hate that subject more than anything. I could not even memorize the multiplication table by heart, and the numbers in a fraction were like jumbled letters to me.

In my first year at CAIC, my algebra teacher was Mr. Aguilar. Prior to his class, I thought that I could just let the subject float and finish my high school math without trouble but without achievements too. But I was wrong for both of my expectations. On the very first day of class, Mr. Aguilar asked the class if we knew the multiplication very well. No one raised a hand, which was not unexpected for me. But what was surprising was the event that followed. Since no one raised their hand, the teacher asked us, one by one, to recite the multiplication table from 1 to

10. Those who could not recite would stand in front of the class. That moment was a nightmare for me because I was so sure

that I could not recite it, not even until its middle. Thankfully, the whole period for the class was already consumed before I was even called. It was a blessing in disguise that I would still have the time to memorize and study the multiplication table.

In his next class, I was finally called, but that time, I successfully recited everything! After all the nervousness that I had on the first day, I mustered the courage and did exceptionally well. After my turn, I could not help but say to myself that it was, in fact, easy. I was so happy that I memorized what I needed, though I still did not learn it by heart. At the end of the class, Mr. Aguilar announced that he would be offering his personal time, between 7:00 a.m. to 8:00 a.m., for the remedial class in Mathematics. He said he would teach the students who were struggling in Math, and so I thought it was a good idea!

Because I was a diligent student and I was determined to overcome my limitations in Math, I attended Mr. Aguilar's remedial classes every day. During our first session, he asked me about the challenging topics for me. I honestly replied and said that I struggled with operations involving fractions, understanding and working on improper fractions, and finding the least common denominator. I also told him about how I could not memorize the multiplication table by heart. My ever so good teacher, Mr. Aguilar, took a pen and paper and explained everything to me. He used plain language so that I could understand the concepts better. Then, he showed me the step-by-step method of answering questions related to the topics. With his guidance, everything just seemed easy and simple. Later that day, Mr. Aguilar gave me homework. It was a good day for me.

When I went home, I felt so happy because finally, I was able to understand the Math topics that I had been struggling with for a long time. I could not explain the kind of relief that Mr. Aguilar gave me that day. After seeing his methods of teaching and his way of encouraging his students, my hope was revitalized, and I was sure that I could finally enjoy Math this time. And so I answered my homework that day. Like magic, the numbers just seemed to make sense that day. I realized that the answers were not that difficult to find after all. Maybe I was just discouraged before that I did not push myself to study the subject harder. Maybe it was also due to the effective explanation that Mr. Aguilar did. Regardless, I was thankful that I was finally enjoying Math for the first time in forever.

The following day, I submitted the assignment to Mr. Aguilar. He went over my answers and gladly told me that I got all the answers right! I was in cloud nine after getting a perfect score, knowing that had I been given the same questions two days ago, I would likely get a failing mark. Mr. Aguilar tapped me on my shoulder, and with a big smile, said that I was a very good student. I think that was the support and encouragement that I always needed.

I could not find an explanation, but after that day, my initial disinterest in Math turned into interest. It was like a 180°. Math became my favorite subject, and it made a whole lot of a difference in my life. I memorized multiplication by heart. I could recite it forward, backward, or from whatever direction, one may like. In my third year in high school, Mr. Aguilar became my geometry teacher too. There, he shared with me the formula of the quadratic equation and also taught me when and how to use it. I learned ratio and proportion from him. I even learned how to apply them in real life, such as when finding missing dimensions of houses, fields, and so on.

Without a doubt, Mr. Aguilar greatly influenced the course of my life. But more than all the math lessons that I learned from him, a word of wisdom that he once shared made the biggest impact. He said that if I understand Algebra and how it works, then I would not have problems in solving engineering problems when I go to college. I was really interested in engineering and was planning to take that course, and Mr. Aguilar's words inspired me to work harder and continually improve my Math skills. He was like a compass that gave a direction to my life.

Aside from the academic requirements, I was also active in extracurricular activities. I had adventures and memorable experiences in all of them, but one stands out from the rest. I was a member of the school's Jr. ROTC at that time. One night, our commander-in-chief called us for a meeting. There, he said that we had to guard the school premises until midnight. I did not know the reasons why, but as an order, we had to comply no matter what. We were assigned in pairs to guard post number 1 and post number 2.

Post number 1 faced the street leading to our house, so I chose that post during my assignment. The nights in Panganiban were always pitch dark. We had no electricity yet, and the only lights aside from the gas lamps were the shining moon and stars. Fortunately, our school had a giant generator that powered lights around its fences. The town was all dark aside from the school. It was expected, though, because that was how it always had been.

Even the students who used the library after class hours already left earlier, knowing how dark the streets were.

And so it was only my partner and me there. He was stationed at post number 2 on the other side of the school perimeter. We were tasked to guard the school until midnight, but for whatever reason, every minute seemed to last an hour! Indeed, time passes slowly when things are boring. There was nothing to see around. All I can hear were the crickets and the other insects making their sounds.

After a seemingly long time, midnight finally came. My partner lived somewhere on the other side of the school where his post was. So, we walked separately in different directions. It was midnight, and obviously, no one was around anymore. Back in those days, we had no gadgets and electricity, so people had to sleep early. I was walking on the very dark streets of Panganiban. I had no flashlight, and it was a moonless night. The only help I had was the stars shining my way. While walking, I was thinking of my exam the next day and was worried that I had not studied yet. I was thinking of how to fit my review in my morning schedule the next day when suddenly, I noticed that something was walking on the other side of the street. It was small, so it was not a man. Looking closely, I realized that it was a little black pig about the height of my knees.

In the '40s, many people still believed in supernatural beings. Even I grew up with stories about fairies, ghosts, gnomes, dwarfs, and other supernatural beings. In the Philippines, we had plenty of local versions too. We had *tiyanak,* a vampiric baby, *manananangal,* a creature with wings that can separate its lower and upper body, *tikbalang,* a half-man, half-horse creature, and so on. The stories of these beings had been a part of Filipino tradition, especially in the early days. I heard of these stories everywhere when I was still a child. For me, I did not know whether I believed them or not, yet still, I found the stories interesting to hear.

It had been a belief that *aswang,* another supernatural being, can take shapes of animals. Some say they can turn into huge black dogs, cats, and pigs. That night, seeing the small black pig on the streets did not give me any hint about it being an *aswang*. And so I continued walking. But after traveling about five yards, I felt as if some steel-brush hair was rubbing my right shoulder. It was a prickling feeling, and when I turned my head to check, I was surprised beyond words upon seeing a huge black pig! I run as fast as I could without looking back. After that encountered, I started believing that *aswangs* really do exist!

I've had the most memorable academic and extracurricular experiences. But of all, I am most proud of this story that happened in my last year in high school. It was my senior year when again, like in Grade 6, I was faced with an important lesson in honesty. That year, I was elected as the treasurer of the Future Farmers Association of the Philippines, an organization including the five provinces of the Bicol Region. That same year, our school was named as the host for the upcoming convention. The students were paid for their fieldwork so that they would have money to contribute and use for the said convention. As a result, the money that was coming into me got bigger and bigger. It was a huge responsibility on my part.

The school was also busy preparing for the event. One time, the school principal gave me a bundle of money to take home and count. He gave me a note containing the amount of the said money and was only tasked to keep the money and to double-check the amount. Two of my classmates volunteered to help me count the money, and so together, we went home. To our surprise, the money that was given by the principal did not tally with the principal's note. We counted repeatedly, but still, there was still an excessed huge amount. My classmates convinced me to just divide the extra money among the three of us and keep it a secret. I firmly said NO!

The following day, I mentioned and gave the principal the excess money as I returned the bundle of money to him. Instantly, he gave me a big smile as if he was expecting to see me do the very same thing. He thanked me, and his words and smile filled my heart. That day, I told myself that I just passed the honesty test!

I did not have the money that I could have taken from the bundle, but my heart was even happier. I owe it to my parents that they taught us the importance of honesty and trained us to apply it to real life. At school, the lesson on honesty was reinforced by my teachers, like how Mrs. Santos asked for honesty from my class in the sixth grade. As a result, I am proud enough that I grew up to be an honest person.

I finished high school as the Class '58 valedictorian. I endured the difficulty of completing my high school's curriculum, excelled in my subjects, and graduated with so much pride because I was honest. When graduation day came, I marched proudly on stage. More than my academic awards, I felt like I was a gem for being honest and for having the right character, honor, and dignity of the man.

After high school graduation, my classmates and I parted separate ways. Some of them started their own families. Others moved to other provinces or cities to seek opportunities. The rest pushed their education even further and attended college. I was part of the latter.

Despite growing up in poverty, I had such a huge dream. I did not want to limit myself, and I wanted to achieve more in life. And so I decided to continue on to college. Using my grades in high school, I applied for a scholarship from a university in Manila. I knew that my family did not have the money to send me to college, so I was really overjoyed when I received a scholarship from Araneta University. I was allowed to complete a five-year Agricultural Engineering course for free! In return, I had to maintain a certain grade so that my scholarship would continue until my college graduation. My sisters Luz and Gloria provided me with financial assistance for my other expenses in school. Thankful as I was for the scholarship and my family's support, I studied really hard and, once again, graduated with Latin honors. I graduated from Araneta University in 1963, earning a degree in Agricultural Engineering.

Looking back on my journey in education, I feel really thankful for all the opportunities that came my way. Having experienced WWII, growing up in poverty, and the challenges that I faced just so I could comply with all the academic requirements from elementary to college, even I find it fascinating how I was able to achieve so much despite the circumstances. I will not attribute my success to pure luck because I know that I also worked really hard for them. Nonetheless, I am thankful for the people and all the supports that I received along the way.

Chapter 12

Inevitably Moving Forward

I cannot be where I am now without the support of the important and influential people in my life. I was the Frank that was born in the wooden hut and was molded by the circumstance that I was born to.

More than anyone, it was my family who gave me the best of everything— memories, experiences, lessons, everything. My Nanay was the first person who made me experience unconditional love. It was her who taught me to be caring and loving to others. My Tatay taught me the practical things in life. He guided me on the farm and taught me the most common livelihood of the time. He also fueled my interest in farming, which I was able to use until the latter parts of my life. My brothers were also a friend to me. We shared fun experiences and adventures together, and they also helped me learn the ins and outs of farming. Like my Nanay, my sisters were loving and caring. My elder sisters took care of me and even supported me during my studies.

I am thankful for having neighbors and relatives that were always ready to help our family when we were in need. I am glad of growing up in a community that offered a helping hand with one another. If they were absent during the most crucial moments of my life, I think I would not be here anymore, writing the story of my life. With God's grace, my relatives and the townspeople saved my life on multiple occasions.

In terms of happiness, my friends, playmates, and co-vaquero in Panganiban made my early life colorful and fun beyond words. Together, we experienced the horrors of WWII. Together, we also found good things that offered us happiness despite the challenges. It was with them that I was able to create memories in almost every part of the town—the fields, mountains, rivers, and the town proper itself. I enjoyed adventures with them, adventures that kids nowadays will not understand.

My classmates and teachers also helped me become who I was now. It was with and because of them that I was trained academically. My teachers reinforced the important life lessons that my parents imparted to me as a child. They played a crucial role in my decisions in life and in my success too.

But like how the book is nearing its end, I also needed to bid farewell to my hometown, Panganiban. After finishing my degree from Araneta University, I worked for a while in the Bureau of Soils in the Philippines before I was admitted at the University of California, Davis, to advance my studies in Agricultural Engineering. I was offered a job as a graduate research assistant at the same department. At that time, I was faced with a huge decision in life. I always had this thirst for knowledge and education, but it also broke my heart thinking about leaving my family and Panganiban behind.

After long contemplation, I came up with the decision to move forward. I realized that I may be leaving my hometown and my family behind, but I know that the relationship and memories would always remain fresh and alive. I may be far from them, but I knew that my heart would forever remain. So, I finalized my decision and continued my enrollment at the University. Fortunately, I had an uncle living in San Francisco, California that time, and I was able to ask for their assistance to help me move to California. They were eager to help.

Aside from my family, I did not inform anyone in town about my departure. I thought that if the trip was postponed or canceled, it would be embarrassing. So, I left Panganiban quietly and with a heavy heart. I knew that I would miss them, especially during my first months or years in the U.S. Still, I had to fight my longing and focused my sight forward. I left Panganiban, my hometown. I left the town that contained all my happy and challenging memories as a child. I boarded Pan American flight # 863 (Fictitious name) on the 22nd of August 1963, leaving the Philippines just a few months after my college graduation. It was my first time traveling through the air, so my emotions were really mixed up. I was sad about leaving my hometown and my country, nervous about being higher than our kites were, and somehow still excited for the new adventures that awaited me. Probably because of my sadness, the flight seemed endless. Until finally, the plane landed. I heard the announcement requesting us to disembark the plane.

With a nervous heart, I put my foot in the airstair until I was on the ground.

I arrived at San Francisco International Airport via Pan American Airlines on the night of the 23rd of August 1963. I immediately noticed the sudden change of temperature as I came from a tropical country and suddenly moved to a temperate one. I was so glad to finally reach my destination. I thought that everything was perfect until I realized that one of my luggage was missing! I immediately asked one of the ticket counter personnel about the luggage's whereabouts only to found out that I left my luggage in Tokyo, Japan, where we had a stopover. I was then informed that the missing luggage would just be delivered to my uncle's address the following day.

While waiting for my uncle, I faced another problem—I felt a call of nature. I looked around, but I did not see any signs leading to a toilet. Out of urgency and frustration, a approached a lady with luggage in her hand and asked her where the comfort room was. To my surprised, she asked me back, "Why, are you sad?" I said that no, I was not sad, but I badly needed to use one. And I guess she understood me better with that and asked if I was looking for the men's restroom. I said yes and hurriedly went over the direction that she pointed at. While using the toilet, I realized that Americans did not use "comfort room" as Filipinos do. Thankfully, the lady was able to understand my dire situation and need!

Finally, my uncle came. I was fetched by the brother of my father, Uncle Andres, who was living in San Francisco since 1954. Upon seeing me, he greeted me and welcome me to San Francisco. I was so delighted beyond words! While driving to 1519-39th

Avenue, I told my uncle the epic story of my arrival, and we laughed our hearts out all the way to our new home. And that was my first day in San Francisco and the first page of another book of my life!

Glossary

Ama	father
Apo sa tuhod	great grandson
Araro	wooden plow operated by man and draft animal
Arbularyo	herbalist or quack doctor; has not undergone medical training
Aswang	a supernatural being that can copy the forms of animals
Asyab	improvised scythe used for harvesting rice
Bahay kubo	nipa hut
Bangus	milkfish
Banka	wooden boat
Be-as	tube container made from bamboo stem with the upper node removed and the lower node acting as the base
Bolo	single-edged knife commonly historically used as a weapon; can also be used in clearing vegetation
Dapdap	a local tree that blooms orange flowers but without leaves
Darikhon	large bamboo cane with one node at the end; placed on the back of animals to carry loads
Gombawa	(Japanese) a form of greeting

Halo-halo	A Filipino dessert prepared by combining several ingredients with crushed ice, sugar, and milk
Ina	mother
Inang	mother
Inay	mother
Kaingin	swidden farming; cutting and burning or land area for agricultural purposes
Karmot	improvised wooden equipment used for harrowing the field
Konitsiwa	(Japanese) a form of greeting
Lambanog	traditional Filipino drink made from distilled palm or nipa sap
Lavandera	washerwoman or laundress; washes clothes for the family or as a livelihood
Lola sa tuhod	great grandmother
Lolo sa tuhod	great grandfather
Lugaw	porridge made from boiled rice
Magtanim ay Di Biro	a traditional Filipino song about the difficulties of planting rice
Manananggal	a supernatural being; can cut his body in half, with wings in the upper body
Namo	a local yam that is poisonous if not sufficiently cooked
Nanay	mother
Ngayangay	a poisonous fish
Noli Me Tangere	(Spanish) Touch Me Not; a novel written by Dr. Jose Rizal against the Spaniards
Ohayo	(Japanese) a form of greeting
Opo	a polite way of saying "yes" in Filipino
Palay	rice grains
Palo-palo	a wooden tool used for laundry

Partera	traditional midwife; has not undergone medical training
Pinipig	cereal-like food made by pounding roasted immature rice
Plangana	basin made from aluminum; used for laundry
Pluma	feather pen
Po	polite expression used by Filipinos when addressing elders or superiors
Powdan	a piece of bamboo placed in the center of the roof of the nipa hut; holds nipa shingles in place
Sapsap	dried fish
Sari-sari store	small convenience store usually built as an extension of the owner's house
Sasa	a type of palm that grows near swamps or coasts
Tatang	father
Tatay	father
Tigpas	scythe with a scabbard
Tikbalang	a half-man, half-horse creature
Tiyanak	supernatural being; a vampiric baby
Tuba	fermented coconut sap
Vaquero	carabao herder

CPSIA information can be obtained
at www.ICGtesting.com
Printed in the USA
BVHW040840151221
623915BV00033B/634/J

9 781734 964554